THE BENCHMARKING MANAGEMENT GUIDE

LIBRARY

AMERICAN SOCIETY FOR INDUSTRIAL SECURITY
1625 PRINCE STREET
ALEXANDRIA, VA 22314
(703) 519-6200

THE BENCHMARKING MANAGEMENT GUIDE

American Productivity & Quality Center

Foreword by
Laura Longmire
Texas Instruments Incorporated

Publisher's Message by
Norman Bodek
Productivity, Inc.

Productivity Press
Portland, Oregon

Productivity Press
P.O. Box 13390
Portland, OR 97213-0390
(503) 235-0600 (telephone)
(503) 235-0909 (fax)

Cover design by Gary Ragaglia
Printed and bound by Maple -Vail Book Manufacturing Group
Printed in the USA

Library of Congress Cataloging-in-Publication Data

The Benchmarking management guide/American Productivity & Quality
    Center; foreword by Laura Longmire.
        p.   cm.
    Rev. ed. of: Planning, organizing, and managing benchmarking activities. 1992.
    Includes bibliographical references.
    ISBN 1-56327-045-5
    1. Benchmarking (Management) — Handbooks, manuals, etc.
    I. American Productivity & Quality Center. II. Planning, organizing, and managing
    benchmarking activities.
    HD62.15.B46   1993
    658.5'62 — dc20   93-9494
                                                                                CIP

94 95 10 9 8 7 6 5 4 3

Dedication

To the Founders, Members, friends, and staff of the American Productivity & Quality Center and the International Benchmarking Clearinghouse

Contents

Publisher's Message

Process benchmarking is one of the most important developments in the last decade of the American quality movement. From the examples of such competitive giants as Xerox, Motorola, Kodak, Milliken, and Texas Instruments, to name a few renowned benchmarkers, organizations across the United States have learned the value of looking to noncompetitor benchmarking partners for new ideas on process improvement. Companies applying the criteria for the Malcolm Baldrige National Quality Award or similar quality challenges discover that benchmarking is a key element of continuous improvement to serve the customer. The potential competitive advantage — and the time saved from reinventing the wheel — are enormous.

Despite this national surge of interest, unfortunately, few companies know what they are doing when they undertake a benchmarking study. To some managers, benchmarking just means industrial tourism — a few superficial, feel-good plant visits to assure the visitors that they are at par with the host company. Others may take the learning/improvement process more seriously, but inundate a benchmarking partner with pages of questions that could have been answered through secondary research. Still others might misconstrue the benchmarking concept and contact competitors for information under an assumed identity. The benchmarking road is full of hazards for the uninformed.

The new *Benchmarking Management Guide* by the American Productivity & Quality Center offers valuable signposts to help practitioners avoid many of the potential pitfalls in benchmarking. As the Preface points out, the *Guide* was created under the auspices of APQC's International Benchmarking Clearing-house specifically as a resource to address the needs of beginning and experienced benchmarkers. The Clearinghouse is the foremost nonprofit benchmarking center in the country, sponsoring a wide range of training, events, and information services related to benchmarking. Benchmarking expert Greg Watson, a vice president of quality with Xerox and the author of *The Benchmarking Workbook* (Productivity Press, 1992), led the team that compiled Section 1 and several other key sections.

Section 1 of the *Benchmarking Management Guide* offers the basic information you need to understand what benchmarking is and is not, and what you need to manage the process effectively. Its many practical sections include

- what skills are needed, with descriptions of benchmarking positions
- what is appropriate legal and ethical conduct during a study
- how to introduce the concept of benchmarking to top management and to employees who will be involved
- what training is required
- how to plan a study
- how to use secondary research effectively
- how to coordinate efforts across an organization
- how to document and track results of studies

Sections 2 through 9 of the *Benchmarking Management Guide* offer additional support for the practitioner. Section 2 describes results of a survey by the Clearinghouse, with cogent data on key questions related to the respondents' experience, including the number of studies undertaken, factors that affect the success or failure of a benchmarking study, steps in the process used, training required, the importance of a team-based approach, and products and services found useful.

Section 3 offers additional background on the ethical aspects of benchmarking — how to avoid legal and moral perils. It also includes basic etiquette and guidelines for behavioral issues. A full copy of the Benchmarking Code of Conduct developed by the International Benchmarking Clearinghouse appears in Appendix A.

Section 4 provides a valuable model for estimating the cost of a benchmarking study, including calculations for time, travel, and other expenses.

Section 5 details the types of training that are useful for leaders and participants, including advice on the time required and a list of providers.

Section 6 offers a comprehensive comparison of various process models for conducting benchmarking, synthesizing them into a meta-model that can be tailored to any organization's needs.

Section 7 describes resources available for secondary research — the "homework" that is so critical to an effective site visit or telephone session. Topics include how to build a basic research capability, use of data bases for business information, and a list of twelve key information sources that can form the foundation of a benchmarking/competitive intelligence library. Addresses for these information sources are included.

Section 8 compares and contrasts the purpose and criteria of the major quality award criteria in the United States, used by many companies as quality improvement guidelines whether or not they are applying for the awards. The section offers an in-depth look at the 1991 and 1992 Baldrige Award criteria, comparing them with criteria for the Deming Prize, the President's Award, NASA's George M. Low Trophy, and the Shingo Prize, as well as with ISO 9000 requirements. The criteria and addresses for information about each award are presented in appendixes following the text.

Section 9 offers an extensive bibliography of books, reports, and articles related to benchmarking and total quality.

Productivity Press is pleased to be able to serve the needs of benchmarkers by publishing high-quality materials to assist with companywide education and implementation. Greg Watson's *Benchmarking Workbook* is a landmark as a practical step-by-step introduction to the benchmarking process. This *Benchmarking Management Guide* is a worthy companion to the *Workbook*, offering indispensable assistance for actually organizing and managing the benchmarking process. No company should venture into benchmarking without the advantage of its advice.

We would like to thank the American Productivity & Quality Center for permitting us to publish this volume. Thanks especially to Carla O'Dell, director of the International Benchmarking Clearinghouse at APQC for project management; Joe Wexler, Total Quality Consulting for editorial assistance; and Larry Lambert, consultant with the APQC Consulting Group and former vice president of Centers Programs at APQC for project assistance and support.

A number of people helped develop the project at Productivity Press. Speical thanks to former vice president Frank Blanch for encouraging and supporting this project; to Karen Jones for developmental editing; to Dorothy Lohmann for editorial management; to David Lennon and Karla Tolbert for production management; to Karla Tolbert and Gayle Joyce for art preparation and composition; and to Gary Ragaglia for cover design.

Norman Bodek
President, Productivity, Inc.

Foreword

In 1989, I first became familiar with the concept of benchmarking. I kept hearing the upper management of Texas Instruments use the word "benchmarking" as something we needed to do; benchmarking, they said, would be a major endeavor for quality improvements. Since the company had been on a quality journey for about nine years, I had the idea that benchmarking was another quality program that we, as managers, needed to endorse and deploy to our people. Many times I wondered if "benchmarking" was the buzzword for quality for the 1990s. While pondering this new term, I was introduced to the concept and process of benchmarking through a peer contact at Xerox.

In an article in *Modern Material Handling* magazine, I read about a material handling practice almost identical to the operation I then managed. As I read the article, I was astounded by the statistics of a near-identical process at Xerox that used basically the same type of equipment. This operation was doing what we were doing, but at three times our productivity rate. How could this be possible?

Fortunately, the Xerox distribution manager's name was listed in the article. After a few phone calls, I was able to share process information with that manager and learn how I could improve my operations. This sharing session resulted in a four-month sharing partnership, and the Xerox manager taught me that what I was doing was benchmarking. Through faxes from the Xerox manager and a copy of Bob Camp's book on benchmarking,* I learned a new method and deployed it to reduce cycle time and increase quality levels within my operation.

---

* Robert C. Camp, *Benchmarking: The Search for Industry Best Practices That Lead to Superior Performance*, Milwaukee: ASQC Quality Press, 1989.

Our management became aware of the improvements I was making and asked me to share the improvement process throughout Texas Instruments' Defense Systems & Electronics Group. By this time, we knew what benchmarking was and that it would be key to our improving processes and achieving our customer satisfaction goal. Is benchmarking a buzzword? No — it is a quality tool that will yield breakthrough improvements and create visions of improvements that were never thought possible.

A feedback report from our first Malcolm Baldrige National Quality Award application identified benchmarking as an area that we needed to improve and use more throughout Texas Instruments. This quality tool is now identified as one of the five key thrusts that Texas Instruments deploys to maintain our fundamental objective: "Customer Satisfaction Through Total Quality." As benchmarking has progressed, we have improved financial processes, design processes, customer satisfaction measurements, teaming and empowerment, and many other business processes. During our 1992 site visit, the Baldrige examiners stated that benchmarking was one of our best practices. Certainly it was an instrumental practice in the process improvements that ultimately won the Baldrige Award for the Defense Systems & Electronic Group, and one that few organizations can afford not to learn about.

This *Benchmarking Management Guide* is the result of more than 87 companies' working together to fulfill a vision of developing a universal benchmarking method that would help improve productivity. As I have always believed that two heads are better than one, this guide should be one of the best educational tools for learning and using benchmarking.

As a guide, this book enables the user to understand how to manage benchmarking within a company, how to teach benchmarking methods, how to deploy benchmarking, and how to implement the "best practices" that will come with benchmarking. The companies involved in preparing this guide shared many success stories to create a single process that combines all the best processes of benchmarking. The following pages contain the "yellow brick road" that leads to successful benchmarking.

Laura Longmire
Benchmarking Champion
Texas Instruments Incorporated

Preface

This book was conceived during a boisterous meeting in July 1991. This was a meeting of the design team of what was to become the American Productivity & Quality Center's International Benchmarking Clearinghouse. About 30 newly ordained benchmarking "champions" from member companies joined a dozen old hands from organizations renowned for their benchmarking prowess.

The job of this team was to identify what the world needed to make benchmarking a powerful addition to the pantheon of quality tools. Their highest priority item was a benchmarking user's guide.

Why a guide? Those new to the benchmarking arena needed assistance to help them organize their efforts and produce the highest return for their organizations. Those members who had been benchmarking awhile — and had been deluged by requests for help from inexperienced (and ill-prepared) benchmarkers — wanted a resource to which they could refer requesters.

After six months of work, a team headed by Greg Watson (then with the Clearinghouse and now a vice president with Xerox) created this *Management Guide*. Our Clearinghouse members have been using the guide for a year, and all of their feedback indicates it has achieved its intended use.

Now, as benchmarking spreads, we want to make the *Management Guide* available to a larger community. We hope it serves you and your benchmarking efforts as well as it continues to serve our Clearinghouse members.

Carla O'Dell, Ph.D.
Director, International Benchmarking Clearinghouse
American Productivity & Quality Center

Acknowledgments

The American Productivity & Quality Center appreciates the assistance of many individuals and organizations in the preparation of the original materials for the guide. Special thanks to the International Benchmarking Clearinghouse Design Steering Committee for their support and participation in the surveys and other aspects of this publication.

Our special appreciation to Joseph Wexler of Total Quality Consulting for serving as coordinating editor for the original project as well as for this new edition, and to Dr. Carla O'Dell, director of the Clearinghouse, Marda Steffey of Career Development, Gregory Watson of Xerox, and Joe Wexler for editorial assistance. Our appreciation to Larry Lambert of the American Productivity & Quality Center for overall management, guidance, and support for this project and to Stephanie Nejame, Craig Tomas, and Vickie J. Williams for production support on the original version of the guide.

Contributors to each section are as follows:

Section 1   Introducing Benchmarking
            Primary author: Gregory H. Watson, Xerox
            Project management: Larry Lambert, APQC
            Documentation: Sara Brill, APQC

Section 2   Industry's Benchmarking Practices: Executive Summary of a Survey by the International Benchmarking Clearinghouse
            Analyst and writer: Todd Lambertus, APCQC
            Survey produced by the IBC Managing Benchmarking Task Force

Design and administration: Larry Lambert, Kevin Prihod, Carla O'Dell, Greg Watson, Bob Dale, and Linda LaCross
Design Steering Committee:
Sam Bookhart, DuPont
Charlie Burke, Compaq
Bob Camp, Xerox
Tony Durham, NCMS
Keith Hunter, Amoco Production
Eric Kennedy, IBM
John Kimberlilng, Amoco Production
Marilyn Murphy, Pacific Gas & Electric
Brenda Richterkessing, MasterCard
Ron Robinson, Harris Corporation
Special thanks to the benchmarkers who completed the survey.

Section 8   Assessing Quality Maturity: Applying Baldrige, Deming, and ISO 9000 Criteria for Internal Assessment
Authors: The Staff of the International Benchmarking Clearinghouse and the American Productivity & Quality Center Consulting Group
Editors: Gregory H. Watson, Xerox, with Joseph H. Wexler, Total Quality Consulting, and Marda Steffey, Career Development

Section 9   A Bibliography of Benchmarking Literature
Researchers and compilers: Joy Holland and Deanna Thompson, APQC

Thanks also to early contributors from the Design Steering Committee, including Sam Bookhart, DuPont; Fred Bowers, Digital Equipment Corporation; Bob Camp, Xerox; Cheryl Drake, SERVISTAR; Joe Figard, Phillips Petroleum, Jim Heidbreder, The James Group; Carolyn Hubble, Chevron; Paul Smith, Hewlett-Packard; and Jim Staker, Strategic Planning Institute.

Section 1
Introducing Benchmarking

The purpose of this volume is to accelerate the introduction of benchmarking into your company's continuous improvement program. This guide was created with the direct support and participation of 87 companies that are concerned about the state of business competitiveness. They want to stay at the forefront of their industries by applying the principles of total quality management (TQM) to their businesses for continuous improvement. Many of these companies already use benchmarking as a process to stay ahead of the competition — and those that aren't using it now are planning to in the near future.

This guide is appropriate for new as well as experienced benchmarkers. To understand the expectations, requirements, and desires of potential customers, the International Benchmarking Clearinghouse conducted several surveys of the membership. The results of these surveys are summarized in Section 2, and the full report is available from the American Productivity & Quality Center (APQC). This study revealed several major findings. One of the most important is that 96 percent of the respondents are planning to increase their benchmarking efforts over the next five years. Another interesting observation is that 83 percent of these companies rank themselves as "still beginners in benchmarking." These companies believe that they could increase their competitive advantage by improving the effectiveness of their benchmarking.

The guide is intended to provide:

- Useful information and background on benchmarking
- A framework for inter-company collaboration
- A common vocabulary for users of the clearinghouse.

This introduction will propose some operational definitions of benchmarking terms, provide an overview of the approach to benchmarking that is taken with the guide, and describe the ways various readers may want to use this guide.

DEFINING BENCHMARKING

Benchmarking has become a common term since it was popularized by Xerox in the 1980s. It has become recognized as an essential ingredient in the success of Malcolm Baldrige National Quality Award winners. Perhaps the simplest way to introduce benchmarking is to answer some of the common questions people have about this concept.

What Is a Benchmark?

There is a distinction between the word *benchmark* and the process of *benchmarking*. The word *benchmark* comes from geographic surveying where it means to take a measurement against a reference point. In the quality improvement lexicon, a benchmark is a "best-in-class" achievement. This achievement then becomes the reference point or recognized standard of excellence against which similar processes are measured.

What Is the Process of Benchmarking?

While a benchmark is a measure, *benchmarking* is a process of measurement. It is a business process that can contribute to achieving competitive advantage. During the creation of the clearinghouse, the members of the Design Steering Committee developed a working definition of benchmarking:

> Benchmarking is the process of continuously comparing and measuring an organization with business leaders anywhere in the world to gain information which will help the organization take action to improve its performance.

Benchmarking is an ongoing measurement and analysis process that compares internal practices, processes, or methodologies with those of other organizations. The purpose of these studies is to identify best practices that may be adapted to a wide range of organizations and provide them with quantum process improvements, which result in increased business performance.

There are two distinct approaches to benchmarking: competitive benchmarking and process benchmarking.

1. *Competitive benchmarking* measures organizational performance against that of competing organizations. Competitive benchmarking tends to concentrate on the relative performance of competitors using a select set of measures.
2. *Process benchmarking* measures discrete process performance and functionality against organizations that lead in those processes. Process benchmarking seeks the best practice for conducting a particular business process after first validating that the performance of that process is, indeed, world class. Once the best practice is identified and under-

stood, then it may be adapted and improved for application to another organization.

The objective of benchmarking is to provide goals for realistic process improvement and an understanding of the changes necessary to facilitate that improvement. Benchmarking contains a bias for action that can lead to breakthrough and continuous improvement projects for products, services, or processes. The results of benchmarking should be increased customer satisfaction and improved competitive position.

What Types of Process Benchmarking Studies Are Done?

Benchmarking is also segmented according to the types of comparisons that are made during a particular study.

There are four types of potential partners for benchmarking studies, and each produces a different value of output suited to different types of comparisons: internal, competitive, industry or functional, and generic.

1. *Internal studies* compare similar operations within different units of an organization. While this simplifies implementation and data access, it yields the lowest potential for significant breakthroughs. An example of an internal study is the comparison of production planning approaches, which use management information systems at various manufacturing sites within a multi-unit business.

2. *Competitive studies* target specific products, processes, or methods used by an organization's direct competitors. This type of study differs from competitive benchmarking in terms of the depth of the study. Competitive benchmarking seeks to establish measures or benchmarks, rather than specific information about what enabled the degree of performance of the targeted competitor. Competitive process studies are usually conducted by a third party to sanitize competitive information, nominalize performance to an agreed-upon base measure, and report case study information that has been approved by the contributing company. Competitive information is exceptionally difficult to obtain due to the concern about disclosure and antitrust issues. In addition, competitive studies measure current performance levels; however, it is almost impossible to release any information about future developments to competitors. Thus, these studies may not produce results that a study

participant could apply to exceed the level of performance found in the competitive environment. An example of a competitive study is the comparison of product distribution methods used to service a common distribution channel.

3. *Functional* or *industry studies* compare similar functions within the same broad industry or compare organizational performance with that of industry leaders. This type of study has a good opportunity to produce breakthrough results and provide significant performance improvement. Because of the potential for industry studies to become available to direct competitors, these studies are typically conducted in the blind through a third party. A variant of the industrywide approach is to target specific companies that sign nondisclosure agreements and hold the results of the study in strict confidence. An example of a functional study is the evaluation of supplier management systems from a sample of companies that cross industry boundaries.

4. *Generic benchmarking* compares work practices or processes that are independent of industry. This method is the most innovative and can result in changed paradigms for reengineering specific operations. An example of generic benchmarking is a study of bar-coding applications from a wide variety of industries (e.g., checkout stands at grocery stores and railroad-car inventory tracking) as a PC-based inventory control and re-ordering system.

What Is Benchmarked?

Process benchmarking studies evaluate business processes or practices that are important to the performance of the organization. The impetus for the study may be identified problem areas, strategic change initiatives, or continuous process improvement efforts. Processes are often selected to be benchmarked because they have a broader scope than business practices and are important for achieving critical success factors (CSFs) in an organization. Business processes, critical success factors, and business practices are defined next.

- *Business processes* are logical combinations of people, equipment, materials, and methods that are organized into work activities to produce a given output. A principle of TQM is that everything done in business is a process. Thus, all business functions consist of nested or interrelated processes and can be viewed in a hierarchical manner. To help clarify this distinction, we will refer to large-scale processes as systems (e.g., manage business); the components of systems as processes (e.g., distribute products); and the components of processes as activities (e.g., package products). See Figure 1-1 for an illustration. Using this decomposition hierarchy, most benchmarking studies are conducted at the activity level. Since the scope of the system and process levels are so broad, the complexity of studies at those levels makes them virtually unmanageable.

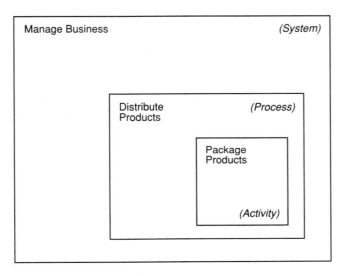

Figure 1-1. Nested Processes

- *Critical success factors (CSFs)* are those characteristics, conditions, or variables that have a direct influence on a customer's satisfaction with a specific business process and therefore on the success of your entire business. CSFs represent the few areas in which satisfactory performance is essential in order for a business to be successful and flourish. It is essential to understand how a particular benchmarking study is going to influence the CSFs of the business. Examples of CSFs include cost reduction, increased shareholder value, and product quality leadership.
- *Business practices* are methods or approaches that facilitate the execution of a process. For example, internal assessment is a business process. A business practice is to base the criteria for internal assessment on the Malcolm Baldrige National Quality Award Criteria. Another business practice is to use ISO 9000 as the standard for assessment of product quality assurance.

An example of these distinctions is on-time introduction and delivery of new products. The development of new product designs is a process, while ensuring that customer input is used to define product features is a practice.

Another factor that limits the scope of benchmarking is the resource requirement. There is no hard and fast rule for what should be benchmarked. Budget and financial prudence on the part of management will emphasize benchmarking for areas of critical importance to the business. A benchmarking study can cost as much as $100,000 or as little as $5,000. Management needs to look at the resources available and decide where the line needs to be drawn between cost versus the potential payback from the study.

Finally, some organizations will select problem processes for benchmarking to eliminate known concerns. Others will select areas that are related to strategic business issues. In any case, "what to benchmark" is an important business decision that must be made consciously. A final consideration of what to benchmark is the quid pro quo nature of benchmarking. This means that an expectation is being set with your benchmarking partners that you will share information with them. Management needs to be aware of external information disclosures to ensure that company trade secrets or competitive information is not disseminated. Many companies have established standard operating procedures to control their sensitive information.

Who Is Benchmarked?

Perhaps the most difficult aspect of a benchmarking study is identifying the appropriate target companies or benchmarking partners. The various classes of companies to be benchmarked were described earlier: internal, competitive, industry or functional, and generic. The key question is how do you identify which particular company should receive the detailed attention of a benchmarking study? The primary tool used to answer this question is secondary research. This is the process of identifying, through literature search and personal contacts, which companies perform the process in an exceptional manner. Industry award winners, functional excellence recognition, and national quality award presentations are three indicators of excellence that help to separate one company from another. However, the truly excellent company may not choose to apply or compete for an award. That company may not want its process excellence to be displayed for all to see. Building a network of personal contacts can lead to the richest sources of organizations to benchmark.

A word of caution is needed. Gaining access at the appropriate level is a critical success factor in conducting benchmarking studies. Some companies that are known for excellent processes, for example, L.L. Bean, Xerox, or Federal Express, have been inundated with requests for benchmarking on the same topic by a variety of companies. These companies have a need to reduce the redundancy in their replies while maintaining a responsive attitude to requests from companies that may be their customers or suppliers. The winners of the Malcolm Baldrige National Quality Award know that they have not achieved "best-in-class" status on every one of their business processes. However, many companies make the mistake of believing that their target benchmarking partner should be a company that has been awarded the Baldrige Award. Selecting the right company and finding the right contact within that company are two of the most troublesome areas for new benchmarkers. Those who are experienced in benchmarking have built their personal network of contacts and work their list to gain access to the process owners within the targeted benchmark partner company.

How Is a Benchmarking Study Completed?

Benchmarking studies can take many forms: telephone surveys, written questionnaires, literature searches, exchange of prepared materials, or site visits. Benchmarking studies generally follow a four-step process: planning a benchmarking project, collecting data, analyzing the data for performance gaps and process enablers, and improving by adapting process enablers.

What Is the Result of a Benchmarking Study?

A benchmarking study may provide outputs. First, it should provide a measure that compares performance for the benchmarked process among the target organizations. Second, it should describe the organization's gap in performance as compared to these identified performance levels. Third, it should identify best practices and enablers that produced these results observed during the study. Finally, the study should set performance goals for the process and identify areas where action can be taken to improve the sponsoring organization's performance. The sponsoring organization is then responsible for implementing the action plan.

What Is a Best Practice?

Best practices are leadership, management, or operational methods or approaches that lead to exceptional performance. Best practice is a relative term, not an absolute standard. Rather than seeking the absolute best, which may not be a cost-effective approach, many benchmarkers optimize by looking for studies with the greatest impact and are satisfied with discovering practices that are innovative, interesting, and identified as contributing to improved performance at leading companies.

What Are Enablers and How Are They Distinct from Best Practice?

Enablers are a broad set of activities that help to enhance the implementation of a best practice. Enablers help to explain the reasons behind the performance indicated by a benchmark measure. Identifying enablers helps to facilitate the transfer of a best practice from one company or organization to another. For example, a particular best practice may relate to the translation of customer product expectations into product attributes. A methodology that aids in this practice is called quality function deployment (QFD). Therefore, QFD is an enabler for this product definition best practice because QFD is used to record customer input and translate it into engineering features. Enablers may not be universal and must be carefully assessed before adapting them for use in a particular company. They may be a principal driver for a best practice while other factors contribute to achieve the best performance level. In the case of this product definition example, concurrent engineering practices and design of experiment methods may also be enablers that augment QFD to facilitate the best practice.

How Have Benchmarking Studies Influenced Organizations?

Benchmarking studies have been used to position companies strategically. Xerox uses benchmarking information to set goals for its principal measures of business performance and has reported significant savings as a result of applying the results of benchmarking studies. Other organizations that have obtained significant successes from benchmarking include Alcoa, AT&T, Digital Equipment Corporation, DuPont, Hewlett-Packard, IBM, Johnson & Johnson,

Kodak, Milliken, Motorola, Texas Instruments, Westinghouse, and Weyer-haeuser. In these cases, the benefit derived from benchmarking is threefold:

1. Building awareness of the best practice for performance in a particular process
2. Learning the measure of excellence for the targeted process
3. Applying these lessons within the sponsoring organization where they can be used to improve performance results

It is not uncommon to achieve savings in the hundreds of thousands of dollars as a result of applying the benchmarking process for continuous improvement. The ratio of results to costs for benchmarking studies can be greater than five to one.

Why an International Clearinghouse for Benchmarking?

A clearinghouse is needed to help foster the use of benchmarking and facilitate the sharing of information and techniques among a wider audience of organizations. The vision for the International Benchmarking Clearinghouse is to provide leadership in promoting, facilitating, and improving benchmarking to improve quality and productivity in organizations throughout the world. Best practices know no border of political, industrial, or geographic dimensions. They may be found in Europe, Japan, or North America; in health care, manufacturing, government, or educational organizations; in democratic, nationalistic, or dictatorial nations. Since the economic borders of the world have been shrinking, the need for competitive awareness on a global perspective has increased. The Clearinghouse meets this need by taking a global approach to benchmarking. While the Clearinghouse is based in the United States, and seeks to improve the competitiveness of American organizations, it is also international, providing services and promoting the use of benchmarking worldwide. This approach recognizes that the improvement of quality and productivity is a win-win situation for every member country of the world's economic community.

How Did the Clearinghouse Originate?

The idea of the Clearinghouse was developed in the spring of 1991. Dr. C. Jackson Grayson, chairman of the American Productivity & Quality Center, invited 23 companies that had been recognized as active in benchmarking or recipients of the Malcolm Baldrige National Quality Award to attend a meeting in Houston to determine the degree of interest. Needless to say, there was a significant degree of interest. The attendees agreed to form a core group to design the type of service needed to facilitate the support of benchmarking in a cross-industry, global context. By November 1991, when this committee's work was completed, 87 companies had joined the Design Steering Committee and were actively participating in organizational work that focused on developing the services of the Clearinghouse.

Why a Benchmarking Management Guide?

The members of the Design Steering Committee conducted several surveys to determine the types and features of services desired by the participants. One service that ranked high on the list was the development of a user's guide to show people how to benchmark. One of the Design Steering Committee's subcommittees, called "Managing Benchmarking," was dedicated to fulfilling this need by producing, reviewing, and editing this work. Designed to provide practical advice on every aspect of benchmarking — from ethics and a code of conduct to the process for benchmarking techniques for analysis and presentation of results — the guide is a basic reference for benchmarking.

USING THIS GUIDE

The benefits to an individual user will depend on his or her understanding and experience in benchmarking.

For the Beginning Benchmarker

Beginning benchmarkers are encouraged to study this manual carefully. The first step in benchmarking, as in the application of most quality processes, is the toughest. By thoroughly understanding benchmarking, a novice benchmarker can be in a better position to promote the development of this process within his or her organization. Pay particular attention to Part I of Section 1, "Getting Started in Benchmarking." This part provides information about how to promote a benchmarking program, the code of conduct for benchmarking, and training programs for management, team members, and general employee orientation.

Part II, "Conducting a Benchmarking Study," describes the implementation of benchmarking and how to support it. Information in this section includes a process model for benchmarking, the relationship of benchmarking to strategic planning, and basic aspects of establishing a benchmarking focal point or program office as the responsible contact point within your company.

Part III, "Building a Benchmarking Organization," provides guidance for the long haul. This section describes the need for developing a benchmarking network, documentation and records maintenance for a benchmarking program, and the process for coordinating study efforts. The later sections of this guide will provide in-depth material that supports the basic text.

For the Experienced Benchmarker

Experienced benchmarkers who are already familiar with the basic text of Section 1 may want to dig into Sections 2 through 9 for detailed information about benchmarking. These sections include:

- the Executive Summary of the Design Steering Committee's benchmarking survey;
- a background paper on the Benchmarking Code of Conduct;
- a cost-analysis model for benchmarking;
- a survey of external benchmarking training;
- an analysis of the benchmarking process models used by 42 members of the Design Steering Committee;
- a paper describing secondary research methods and data sources;
- a report comparing internal assessment systems and stressing the power of secondary research and information gathering; and
- a bibliography of benchmarking-related books, reports, and articles.

Part I
Getting Started in Benchmarking

INTRODUCTION

This section of the guide addresses issues that face companies as they begin their benchmarking activities. Benchmarking is a continuous learning process. Lessons are identified from organizations whose performance is admired, and then those lessons are applied within your own organization. Beginning this cycle requires management support, employee involvement, and process-owner participation. The process for obtaining support, involvement, and participation follows a five-phase approach:

1. Understanding the behaviors and protocol of benchmarking
2. Planning for the implementation of benchmarking
3. Developing the skills required to facilitate benchmarking studies
4. Training both managers and employees in the skills they need to participate in, interpret the meaning of, and apply the results of benchmarking studies
5. Communicating clear expectations of the benchmarking services provided and establishing the organization's responsibility for participation

While this section is heavy on education and training support for benchmarking, please remember Dr. Kaoru Ishikawa's observation that "quality begins and ends with education." Both education and training help to accelerate the process learning curve for participants by exposing them to the experience of those who have pioneered the way.

This guide has profited by the experience of those early American benchmarkers at Alcoa, AT&T, Boeing, Digital Equipment Corporation, DuPont, General Electric, General Motors, Hewlett-Packard, IBM, Johnson & Johnson, Kodak, Milliken, Motorola, Texas Instruments, Westinghouse, Weyerhaeuser, and especially Xerox. These companies have recognized the value of benchmarking for continuous improvement and the need for benchmark information to support their business planning process.

The lessons of this first section of the guide come from the early efforts of these companies to develop protocols and expectations around a new model for American business: a cooperative model of sharing across industrial boundaries.

BENCHMARKING PROTOCOL AND THE CODE OF CONDUCT

There are many concerns about sharing information among companies. For instance, there are the legal issues of potential antitrust violations that could occur among companies from the same industry. There are practical issues of protecting company private information and the need for developing mutually acceptable nondisclosure agreements. There are also moral issues about the degree of preparation for benchmarking exchange meetings. To help establish some of the legal, moral, and ethical conventions that have been informally practiced among benchmarkers, the Clearinghouse and the Council on Benchmarking of the Strategic Planning Institute have jointly developed a Code of Conduct to guide the relations among benchmarkers.

This jointly developed code is a brief document. The Clearinghouse uses an expanded version of this code, which is included in Section 3, "Applying Moral and Legal Considerations to Benchmarking Protocol." The expanded version is inclusive of the joint code. While Section 3 provides a detailed description of the code and related issues, a summary is presented here. The essential elements of the Code of Conduct include the following guidance:

- Keep it legal.
- Be willing to give what you get.
- Respect confidentiality.
- Keep information internal.
- Use benchmarking contacts.
- Don't refer without permission.
- Be prepared from the start.

- Understand expectations.
- Act in accordance with expectations.
- Be honest.
- Follow through with commitments.

The principles of the Code of Conduct seek to avoid behavioral issues such as poor stewardship of intellectual property, antitrust violations or unfair trade practices, conflicts of interest, and trade libel disparagement. Many of these concerns arise from dealing with direct competitors. In general, it is reasonably safe to have occasional direct contact with competitors regarding business functions that are not directly responsible for market conditions. To present an example, the following do not represent risk areas for competitive dialogue:

- Quality programs and methods
- Human resource management and personnel issues
- Employee safety and health areas
- Facilities management
- Internal auditing practices
- Purchasing and supplier management
- Facilities management
- Legal processes and political lobbying efforts
- Employee training and development

It is always helpful to establish the ground rules for specific benchmarking engagements up front with your partner. This is particularly true of interactions with competitors. The focus of a benchmarking effort with a competitor should be on areas that do not influence your relative competitive advantage, but on areas where both parties can mutually improve.

Another practice that is helpful is to use an ethical third party to assemble and "blind" the inputs. In addition, it is always advisable to seek the guidance of your company's legal counsel. If you have particular concerns regarding the sharing process, then the following litmus test is proposed for evaluating any resistance that your conscience may be developing:

1. What does your information source expect you to do with the information?
2. Are you asking for information that you would not be willing to provide under similar circumstances?
3. What is the motivation for requesting this information?

4. Can the legitimate objectives of your benchmarking study be met by showing nominalized ratio data, rather than specific data that could be considered proprietary or potentially compromising?
5. Would your request for information or your interactions with a competitor hold up in the light of day? Would you be embarrassed if it were reported in the *Wall Street Journal*?

The Benchmarking Code of Conduct is the essential foundation for benchmarking. Understanding and practicing the behavior and protocol guidelines of benchmarking, as described by this code, is fundamental for individuals who are participating in benchmarking projects. The Code of Conduct is so important for benchmarking that it should be taught to both business managers and professional practitioners of benchmarking.

The code is a living document, as is any professional standard. If you believe that the code needs to be modified, or if you have observed situations that the code does not address, please contact the Clearinghouse staff. We will review your concerns and present them to the members of the Clearinghouse for resolution. It is the intention of the staff and the membership of the Clearinghouse to help practitioners maintain the highest standards of conduct in all professional exchanges.

BENCHMARKING IMPLEMENTATION PLAN

While the Code of Conduct provides a basis for benchmarking relationships, it will not implement benchmarking within your organization. Implementing benchmarking requires a modification of your organization's approach to managing strategic change. Benchmarking is about the managed introduction of change into an organization. Change can be motivated by internal pressures created by the leadership of the organization in response to their vision and goals for future development, or it can be motivated as a reactive response to external pressures from legislative, regulatory, technological, or competitive sources.

In a leadership company, the change-driving force is predominantly internal. To manage change, the organization's leadership must measure and monitor the current performance trends and changing competitive position. This examination is part of the strategic planning process for many companies. Such companies can apply benchmarks for goal determination and performance comparison. Benchmarking provides an external perspective on the validity of internal measures.

The strategic application of benchmarking is quickly accepted by the senior management of most companies. The three areas where senior managers tend to request initial benchmarks are

1. Manufacturing cost overhead analysis
2. New product development cycle time
3. Customer satisfaction improvement

One way to influence senior management support for benchmarking is to suggest a pilot project in the area that has their highest interest.

How should benchmarking be introduced into an organization? Benchmarking should receive a top-down introduction if it is going to have the greatest effect on your organization's business. This means that the implementation should follow a pilot project as suggested by the following steps:

Step 1: Expose senior management to the concepts of benchmarking by presenting the features and benefits of process benchmarking. This may be done in one-on-one discussions with key executives or as a presentation to the senior management team. In either case the objective is to develop sufficient interest in the potential benefits of benchmarking to gain top-management support in conducting a pilot project. Ask that senior managers place the owner of the process that is to be benchmarked on the benchmarking team. Also, establish regular review points for the project with the management team. The content of this executive briefing is described later in this section under the heading "Executive Presentation on Benchmarking."

Step 2: Develop a project cost estimate using the model provided in Section 4, "Analyzing the Cost of Benchmarking Studies: A Model for Comparison."

Step 3: Conduct the pilot project in a way that ensures its success. Obtain training for the process owner and team members. Provide an experienced facilitator to guide the team through the benchmarking process.

Step 4: Ensure that the pilot project follows a rigorous process:

- Identify the customers of the pilot project and understand their expectations
- Establish a clearly defined project purpose and process definition

- Solicit the participation and advice of your organization's legal counsel, in particular for the review of nondisclosure agreements
- Plan the project to provide objective results
- Inform the team of the Benchmarking Protocol and Code of Conduct
- Follow an accepted process model for benchmarking
- Validate your questionnaire or interview guide prior to distribution
- Present nominalized results for process measures
- Develop case studies for potential best practices observed
- Ensure the analyses, conclusions, and recommendations are justified by data

Step 5: Report both the interim and final results of the project to senior management. At the final presentation request those resources necessary to implement the recommended results.

Step 6: Facilitate the implementation of the process change recommended by the study.

Step 7: Monitor the results of the implementation to ensure that they follow the projected results of the pilot project.

After completing this pilot project, develop an implementation plan for a permanent benchmarking activity or program management office, and present that plan to the senior management team. This benchmarking implementation plan describes the actions necessary to integrate the benchmarking process into the business practices of your organization. The plan for implementing benchmarking should include the following details:

- Mission statement for the benchmarking activity
- Position descriptions for staffing the activity
- Process model that will be used for benchmarking
- Training and development requirements for supporting benchmarking
- Documentation handling, storage, and retrieval procedures
- Approval process and designation authority for participating in a benchmarking project
- Priority of desired benchmarking projects by subject area
- Specific requirements for disclosure of information to external companies (legal review)

The specific elements of the implementation plan should be defined in the organization's training materials and procedural documentation for conducting a benchmarking project (the content of a benchmarking procedure will be addressed in Part III).

BENCHMARKING SKILLS

If a company decides that it wants benchmarking to be part of its long-term management program, then it will need to find a way to institutionalize the processes. A permanent benchmarking activity needs to be administered through a program office. The following requirements of this office may be included in its mission statement:

- Plan and coordinate all management-sponsored benchmarking activities
- Sponsor training for benchmarking teams
- Communicate benchmarking activities through newsletters, seminars, and symposiums
- Develop and maintain a technical benchmarking library
- Develop and maintain a data base of benchmarking studies and trip reports
- Manage the budget for benchmarking activities

The principal role of a benchmarking manager is to coordinate all of these benchmarking activities and provide the infrastructure for the daily management of the benchmarking activity. The principal role of a permanent benchmarking professional is to serve as an internal consultant to the rest of the organization and facilitate their progress in benchmarking studies. Specific position descriptions for these two positions are included in Part III. The roles for these positions require that certain skills be developed or recruited in individuals in these areas.

Skills and Characteristics of Benchmarking Managers

This list of skills assumes the need to develop a manager who is not an experienced benchmarking professional, but it also includes the skills recommended for an established benchmarking professional.

- Ability to interact with senior management
- Negotiation skills
- Strong written, verbal, analytical, and presentation skills

- Broad business management experience
- Problem-solving skills and practice in TQM principles and methods
- Project management skills
- Cost center management skills
- Functional expertise in at least one of the key business process areas

Skills and Characteristics of Benchmarking Professionals

Two vocational levels for benchmarking professionals may be identified: one position for a senior-level professional, and the other position for a mid-level professional. Most companies do not use entry-level individuals for professional benchmarking positions. The following list contains the skills and characteristics needed by benchmarking professionals.

- Broad business process knowledge and process management skills
- Meeting management and interpersonal communication skills
- Problem-solving skills and knowledge of TQM principles
- Team facilitation and process consulting skills
- Questionnaire and survey development experience
- Interviewing techniques and experience
- Tool skills for analytical thinking and presentation
- Written- and verbal-communication ability and presentation skills
- Diplomatic approach with senior managers

EXECUTIVE PRESENTATION ON BENCHMARKING

As with any sales presentation, you must know your audience before briefing senior managers. Most senior managers are concerned about the translation of their strategic goals and business objectives into reality.

Benchmarking can help facilitate their translation by providing concrete examples of other companies that have made similar transformations. Some of these companies include the Xerox copier products division, Ford's Team Taurus, and Hewlett-Packard's 10X program for hardware quality improvement. These examples help to overcome resistance to change by removing a barrier of uncertainty that is raised around the ability to achieve "stretch" goals. As the *Wall Street Journal* reported (August 20, 1991), a survey found that 62 percent of chief executives seek advice from their senior management team, 56 percent consult their board of directors, but only 25 percent go outside their company to talk with colleagues in their fields.

Benchmarking provides a structured approach for senior managers to discover what is going on outside their organization.

The scope of benchmarking involvement for senior management does not need to extend to all business processes that define their enterprise. While all business processes are important to the functioning of a business, some are more critical to the business operation. These key business processes represent core functional efforts and are usually characterized by transactions that directly or indirectly influence the external customer's perception of the organization. For instance, Xerox management has stated that they have identified 11 key business processes, while IBM management has identified 16.

These processes represent cross-functional areas where the organization must excel to maintain its competitive position. Benchmarking of these key business processes should receive the sponsorship of senior management. Developing a business process taxonomy (see Part II) will help you to identify the specific key business processes of your organization.

While senior managers do not have to be involved in all benchmarking processes, they do need to provide leadership to the benchmarking program by:

- Emphasizing the need for benchmarking
- Ensuring that adequate education and training is provided to the benchmarking team
- Selecting the team leader and providing members of the team with the time to conduct their benchmarking project
- Setting the resource and information-sharing boundaries within which benchmarking efforts take place
- Making peer-to-peer contacts with other companies to initiate conversations about benchmarking
- Providing the resources, time, and support required to do a quality job
- Receiving the results and recommendations of the project with an open mind, making every effort to implement the most important results
- Recognizing the efforts of benchmarking teams for their contributions

An effective presentation to senior management about benchmarking needs to explain the benchmarking process, the benefits of benchmarking, the resources required for process benchmarking, and management's role in benchmarking. All of this needs to be accomplished within an hour to an hour and a half. Several member companies of the Design Steering Committee submitted copies of their executive-level benchmarking presentations for the Clearing-house research library. From those briefings, the following outline for a senior management benchmarking presentation was developed:

- Define benchmarks, benchmarking, critical success factors, and enablers
- Explain the objective of benchmarking
- Compare benchmarking with other competitive practices that may be more familiar to them: reverse engineering, competitive product analysis, market research, and industry analysis
- Describe the benchmarking process using a process model
- Walk through the process model by using questions that need to be considered at each step
- Address the issue of what to benchmark — critical success factors in search of enablers
- Provide examples of areas that could be benchmarked
- Describe the results of a successful benchmarking case from a recognized leader
- Illustrate the use of benchmark data for setting strategic goals
- Demonstrate how benchmarking can be integrated with strategic planning to encourage effective change initiatives
- Define the elements of a benchmarking program: organization, approach to conducting studies, and the proposed relationship with potentially overlapping business areas in market research, product engineering, and the corporate library
- Specify the request that you want senior management to consider, whether it is to sponsor a pilot study or to provide resources to initiate a benchmarking program office

EMPLOYEE ORIENTATION TO BENCHMARKING

The purpose of an employee orientation is to inform employees about the benchmarking program and to enable them to participate on a facilitated benchmarking team or on a team that is implementing the results of a benchmarking project. This orientation is not intended as skill training that would produce employees who are capable of conducting an unfacilitated benchmarking project. The employee orientation can take the form of a presentation or a booklet that describes benchmarking. The slide or overhead-based presentation format typically lasts four hours. It prepares employees to:

- Define benchmarking
- Recognize the importance of benchmarking
- Recognize the steps involved in conducting a benchmarking project
- Give several examples of previously conducted benchmarking projects
- Recognize the relationship of benchmarking and the organization's quality processes
- Explain how benchmarking is integrated into the planning process
- Read and interpret the results of benchmarking analyses
- Participate in action teams to implement the lessons learned from benchmarking

While using a booklet to describe benchmarking is more expensive than conducting a small number of presentations, for a large organization it may prove to be a cost-effective approach for informing the organization about benchmarking.

The following example of a table of contents was adapted from several examples of introductory booklets that averaged 30 pages in length:

1. Executive foreword: competitiveness and strategic change
2. Overview of benchmarking
3. Definition of benchmarking
4. Value and benefits of benchmarking
5. The benchmarking process
6. Examples of benchmarking projects
7. Description of your organization's benchmarking program
8. Identification of contacts for further information or training

Either of these approaches to communicating about the services and capabilities of your benchmarking program can be effective. One word of caution: don't advertise what you don't have. Once you advertise or promote the concept of benchmarking, you will be surprised at the degree of interest.

Benchmarking is an exciting topic to many managers who see it as a way to encourage improvement among their employees. If you do not have the resources to support benchmarking for your entire organization, then you will need to disclose the limits of the support that you are prepared to offer. It is possible to create some problems by attempting to get into benchmarking more quickly than the organization is able to facilitate and support. One symptom of this condition is "runaway benchmarking." This condition exists when teams from different parts of the organization develop their own support mechanisms and conduct their own projects without the monitoring or support of a formal organization. This condition has several adverse effects:

- Management will have incomplete knowledge of their benchmarking activities and what information is being shared with external organizations.
- Teams may not follow the accepted protocol for benchmarking, and your organization's overall benchmarking effort may be diluted by inappropriate contacts with potential benchmarking partners.
- Teams may not select the most significant projects for benchmarking.
- Teams may duplicate project efforts and resources if they are not coordinated.
- Benchmarking visits may tend to be "plant tours" rather than data-gathering missions.
- Results may not be recorded or shared among teams with related problems or concerns.
- Teams may select training programs that are incompatible with a common approach to benchmarking.
- It will not be possible to track expenses and benefits of organization-wide benchmarking efforts.

BENCHMARKING TRAINING PROGRAMS

Benchmarking training may be found in the form of seminars and workshops or conferences. Training that develops the basic skills for benchmarking is available in one- to three-day sessions. This general skills training in benchmarking is available from a wide variety of sources. Section 5 of this guide provides an overview of benchmarking skill training. Some companies may want to develop their own classes on benchmarking that complement their TQM processes. Course developers and other studious individuals will find help in Section 9, "A Bibliography of Benchmarking Literature," which includes books, reports, and articles about benchmarking.

Through the Clearinghouse, the APQC offers three benchmarking courses to its member companies. The following agendas describe the content of these courses.

"The Basics of Benchmarking": This two-day course is intended to provide an introduction to benchmarking for individuals who have not conducted a benchmarking study. The course describes a general process model for benchmarking and provides detailed information on where to look for data and data-collection forms to encourage progress through each of the four steps of the generic benchmarking model. A case study is used to simulate a real-world benchmarking project.

After completion of this course, the participant will be able to serve successfully as a team member in a benchmarking study project. Specific topics in this course include:

• Definition of benchmarking
• How to determine what to benchmark
• Code of Conduct and protocol for benchmarking
• Benchmarking process model with case study applications
• Projecting the results of gap analysis into corporate "stretch" objectives
• Cultural adaptation of benchmarking study results
• Developing an implementation plan for benchmarking study results

"Applying Advanced Benchmarking Techniques": This two-day course provides experienced benchmarkers with detailed applications of analysis tools used to support the benchmarking process. The topics highlighted in this class are:

• Developing an instrument for telephone, mail, or interview surveys
• Selecting key words for data base searches and conducting secondary research
• Performing analyses of survey results
• Using advanced methods of process analysis and measurement: creating a taxonomy of organizations and measures
• Converting performance gaps into achievable organizational goals

"Organizing and Managing Benchmarking": This one-day course is intended for those individuals charged with implementing process benchmarking within their company. Participants will complete the course by developing a template to introduce benchmarking within their organizations. Topics include:

• Obtaining management support for implementation of benchmarking
• Developing a benchmarking process model

- Understanding legal and ethical considerations for establishing a benchmarking activity
- Organizing for companywide benchmarking: structure and infrastructure options
- Creating organizational charters, benchmarking procedures, and job descriptions
- Training teams and individuals in benchmarking methods
- Developing an information repository for benchmarking and competitive analysis materials

PROMOTING BENCHMARKING SERVICES WITHIN YOUR ORGANIZATION

It is important to clearly communicate the benchmarking services provided by your benchmarking program office. This sets explicit expectations both for services provided and levels of service, and it establishes the rest of the organization's responsibility to participate.

Once your benchmarking efforts have become mature, your organization may want to extend its promotional efforts beyond the executive presentation and employee orientation. Some of the more experienced benchmarking programs feature a variety of communication vehicles designed to improve their benchmarking processes, increase the sharing of project results, and develop improved methods of conducting benchmarking projects. Some of the communication vehicles used by these experienced organizations include:

- Brochures advertising the services of a centralized benchmarking group
- Reminder card or planning calendar insert to summarize the benchmarking process
- Newsletter to describe current projects and case studies, announce group meetings, call attention to the latest benchmarking publications, and describe organizational benchmarking policies
- Benchmarking network of individuals who meet at an annual symposium to share information on their projects and new approaches that have been developed
- Electronic networks for sharing project status, historical study results, and contact lists for initiating benchmarking studies

Part II
Conducting a
Benchmarking Study

INTRODUCTION

Over half of the *Fortune* 500 companies claim to be benchmarking. It has always been an implicit aspect of any business activity; however, benchmarking as a rigorous process within the strategy development process is a fairly recent activity. Because benchmarking is a recent activity, there has been no accepted general practice for conducting a benchmarking study. This section of the guide provides a detailed overview of the benchmarking process to establish a general approach to benchmarking. This section:

- Describes the linkage between strategic planning and benchmarking
- Identifies a generic approach to the benchmarking process and defines its activities
- Presents a set of processes for consideration as topics for benchmarking studies
- Proposes a general template for the description of a business process
- Lists business and process performance measures
- Illustrates the concepts of baseline, entitlement, and benchmarks for process measures
- Introduces the concept of a study plan for managing a benchmarking project
- Describes how secondary research methods can apply to benchmarking
- Presents the elements of a nondisclosure agreement
- Discusses methods for developing surveys, questionnaires, and interview guides

- Provides an interpretation of a gap analysis or "Z" chart
- Presents an approach for developing action plans and implementation plans

BENCHMARKING AND STRATEGIC PLANNING

The fundamental question of strategic analysis is "What does it take to win in this business?" Benchmarking helps to answer this question. The output of a benchmarking study is a description of both how much to improve and how to improve. Benchmarking takes the measure of difference between companies, determines the cause for that distinction, and proposes alternatives to eliminate the distinction. There are several differences between benchmarking, which seeks both a measurable difference and a cause, and competitive analysis, which looks only at measurable differences.

Competitive analysis seeks to answer resource and market-strategy questions about competitors. It seeks out the strengths and weaknesses of the competitors to determine their future threats as well as opportunities. Competitive analysis is usually conducted independent of the strategic plan. It focuses on competitors only and does not compare results with internal measures or develop a plan for using the information gathered.

Benchmarking, however, is tied into the strategic plan. It provides quantifiable internal analysis as well as valid external comparisons. It develops comparisons against the worldwide best-in-class and thereby provides an opportunity to exceed the competition. Finally, benchmarking develops action plans for implementing the results of the study.

The strategic intent of an organization is its long-term focus. This intent is seen in the vision of its management and the cultural values of the organization. The strategic change model presented in Figure 1-2 describes an organization as three levels. The role of senior management is to develop a long-range perspective of the organization's direction and guide the organization in that direction by negotiating the goals of the organization with middle management and reviewing the performance of the implementation teams. While management sets the objectives, each level of the organization participates in the execution. Through the review process the teams provide input for the next level of objective setting. This model requires benchmarking to provide reality to the direction-setting process.

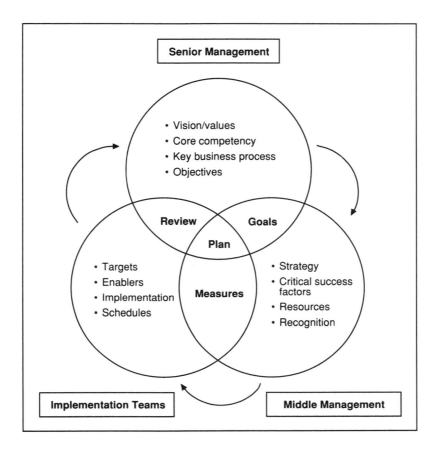

Figure 1-2. Strategic Change Model

The objective of the strategic decision maker is to use strategic analysis, competitive analysis, customer analysis, and process benchmarking as a set of interrelated processes that provide a growth opportunity for the business. Working together, these processes can break down business performance barriers.

To effectively monitor the business requires a strategic-level scan of the business environment: competitors, regulatory agencies, major accounts, critical suppliers, stock-market analysts, etc. By linking together all of the information management systems and data sources, senior management can have the best picture possible for deciding on the future course of business and breaking through performance barriers (see Figure 1-3).

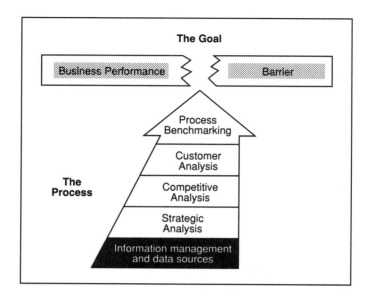

Figure 1-3. Benchmarking to Break Performance Barriers

BENCHMARKING PROCESS MODEL

A process model for benchmarking outlines the steps that are followed during a project. Motorola has a five-step model; Florida Power & Light has a seven-step model; AT&T has a nine-step model; Xerox has a ten-step model.

The number of steps is not as important as the use of an integrated, systematic, measured approach to benchmarking. Section 6, "Comparing Process Models for Benchmarking," contains an analysis of benchmarking process models and proposes a four-step model as a generic approach to benchmarking. The four steps — plan, collect, analyze, and improve — are described on the following pages.

Planning a Benchmarking Project

The objective of the planning phase of benchmarking is to determine what to benchmark and who to benchmark. The specific steps followed during this phase include:

- Select the processes to benchmark
- Gain participation of the process owner

- Select the leader for the benchmarking team and identify the team members
- Identify the process customers' profiles and set of expectations
- Analyze process flow and process performance measures
- Clearly define the process inputs and outputs
- Document and flow diagram the process
- Select the critical success factors to benchmark
- Establish the data-collection method
- Develop the preliminary questionnaire

Information describing this benchmarking project should be recorded on a benchmarking study plan. An example of the information included in this form is presented in Figure 1-4. Notice that the form summarizes the target process definition, lists all significant process measures, identifies the team members and their commitment, states the study objective and approach, and announces the study milestones. This information may be shared using a benchmarking newsletter or electronic bulletin board. Sharing the benchmarking study plan helps to reduce the possibility of duplicated study effort and provides an opportunity to develop synergy among related study projects.

This step ends by developing a preliminary questionnaire. This questionnaire helps to guide the definition of data-collection requirements and also defines the scope of the study for the team.

Collecting Data

The objective of the data-collection phase of benchmarking is to gather information about the target process and companies from both secondary and primary sources. The specific steps followed during this phase of benchmarking include:

- Collect internal process data
- Research similar processes through secondary sources
- Identify best-in-class and potential benchmarking partners
- Plan data collection
- Develop survey or interview guide
- Contact benchmarking partners and gain participation
- Collect preliminary data
- Make on-site observations

Benchmarking Study Plan

Study Topic: Process Owner: Study Sponsor: Team Facilitator:		Date Initiated: Target Completion Date: Review Dates:		
Process Description (Attach Flowchart):				
Suppliers	Inputs	Transactions	Outputs	Customers
Process Performance Measures:				
Critical Success Factors CSF Measures Past CSF Level/Date Current CSF Level/Date Desired CSF Level/Goal Trend Analysis Key Activities Influencing CSF				
Study Team Members:				
Name	Department	Telephone	Role	Time Commitment
Study Objective:				
Study Approach:				
Generic Process Performance Measure:				
Key Study Milestones				

Figure 1-4. Benchmarking Study Plan

The approach to collecting data is recorded in a data-collection plan (see Figure 1-5). This information helps to guide secondary and primary research efforts. Secondary research is conducted by reviewing open literature from journals, newspapers, and conferences to discover what has been revealed to the general public. The information forms a foundation for seeking additional, more detailed information through a telephone interview, mailed survey, or site visit. The preliminary questionnaire developed during the study planning serves as the basis for both the data collection plan and the final questionnaire instrument.

Analyzing Data for Performance Gaps and Enablers

The objectives of the third phase of benchmarking are to quantify the degree of performance gap that exists between your own organization and the process leader and to identify process enablers that provide potential actions to help your organization improve its performance. Additional information on analyzing results is provided in the subsection titled "Data Analysis Methods for Benchmarking" (pages 48-53). The specific steps followed in this phase of benchmarking include:

- Organize and reformat the data to permit identification of performance gaps
- Normalize performance to a common base
- Compare current performance against the benchmark
- Identify performance gaps and their root causes
- Project performance three to five years into the future
- Develop "best practice" case studies
- Isolate process enablers that correlate to process improvements
- Evaluate the nature of the process enablers and best practices to determine their adaptability to your culture

Two worksheets can be used to record information. The first worksheet is the benchmarking results summary (Figure 1-6). This form records the organization-to-organization comparisons with each of the benchmarking partners. The bottom half of the form is used to develop a narrative log of the improvement actions, time frame, and results obtained from the benchmarking partner's improvement efforts. The last section of this narrative should include the

Data Collection Plan

	Subject Matter Experts		
	Name	Department	Phone
Study Topic:			
Plan Date:			

Method Chosen: Secondary Research ☐ Telephone Interview ☐ Mail Survey ☐ Site Visit ☐ Other ☐				
	Generate Questions	Develop Instrument	Pilot/Revise	Finalize
Designer/Developer Completion Date				

Content Analysis and Collection Plan

Topic	Data Required	Information Source	Interviewer/ Collector	Due Date	Complete

Figure 1-5. Data Collection Plan

current plans and expected results over the target time frame for ongoing process improvement activities.

The second worksheet is a performance comparison worksheet (Figure 1-7) used to record the information from the primary companies used in the gap analysis. The companies recorded here are the subset of benchmarking partners whose process performance exceeds your own organization's performance. Up to three process measures may be compared: one indicating overall process performance results (productivity), one indicating process efficiency (cycle time), and one indicating process effectiveness (quality). If cost information is available, it may be recorded in the additional information section. This information is gathered from the set of benchmarking results described for the previous worksheet.

Improving by Adapting Process Enablers and Best Practices

The objective of this final phase of benchmarking is to transfer the learning from the study into improved business processes. This step is further described in the subsection titled "Action Planning and Tracking" (page 53). The specific steps followed in this phase of benchmarking include

- Set goals to reduce, meet, and then exceed the performance gap
- Modify process enablers and best practices to meet your company culture and organizational structure
- Gain acceptance, support, commitment, and ownership for changes required
- Develop an action plan
- Communicate the plan to management for endorsement
- Commit the resources required for implementation
- Celebrate the results of the benchmarking project
- Implement the action plan
- Monitor and report progress toward the goal
- Identify opportunities for future benchmarking
- Recalibrate the measure regularly

The benchmarking action plan (page 54) is used to define the particular project for process improvement, while the benchmarking implementation plan (page 55) is used to track progress of the project as it develops.

Process Name:
Process Owner:
Performance Measure:
Benchmark Company:
Benchmark Improvement Trend:
Process Enablers:

Our Company's Achievement

Our Company's Entitlement

Benchmark Performance

Our Company's Commitment

Level of Performance (Scale)

Time Frame (Scale)

Action	Time Frame	Results

Figure 1-6. Benchmarking Results Summary

Performance Comparison Worksheet

Study Topic:	Performance (Performance Gap: Difference compared to own performance.)			
Metrics Circle Output – Overall Process Performance (O) or Process (P), and Effectiveness (E) or Efficiency (e)	Own Company:	Company A:	Company B:	Company C:
Metric (O/P, E/e):		Gap:	Gap:	Gap:
Metric (O/P, E/e):		Gap:	Gap:	Gap:
Metric (O/P, E/e):		Gap:	Gap:	Gap:
Reasons for Gap: (Environment-Situational Variables, Strategy or Practices)				
Additional Information Required:				

Figure 1-7. Performance Comparison Worksheet

BENCHMARKING PROCESS TAXONOMY

A business can be seen as a system of processes. At the highest level, there are several major processes, each of which can be decomposed into other processes. Business can be viewed as a taxonomy, or structured relationship, among processes. This hierarchical view of business fails to capture the cross-functional nature of many processes. It is precisely the cross-functional processes that must be performed well for a business to succeed. This is an area where benchmarking can be used as a tool for evaluating corporate strategy. It is also an area that needs to have more work performed to fully understand how to build the cross-functional relationships into a hierarchical model.

Benchmarking can be resource consuming since it is a commitment to the continuous monitoring and analyses of business process performance. Many companies that benchmark have found a need to focus their efforts on those few areas that represent the core competencies of the business. A core competency must meet three tests:

1. It must have a wide application in the company's business.
2. It should make a significant contribution to benefits perceived by the customer.
3. It should be difficult for a competitor to imitate.

Some of the processes that may be considered core competencies and thus represent a set of processes for consideration as topics for benchmarking studies, include:

- Product development process
- Customer service process
- Product requirements analysis process
- Supplier management process
- Product sales forecasting process
- Product manufacturing process
- Product distribution process
- Customer complaint handling process

Section 6, "Comparing Process Models for Benchmarking," provides a description of process taxonomy in a broader sense for benchmarking applications and is a starting point for further discussions of process taxonomy.

BENCHMARKING PROCESS TEMPLATE

Benchmarking requires an ongoing monitoring of process performance to recalibrate the process model. This is necessary because of changing industry dynamics that result in new measures of performance, shifting positions among the world's business leaders, and improvement among competitors. Self-monitoring or self-assessment is also required to check if the approach selected was correct and if it was executed correctly. One way to monitor these trends is to maintain a chart of benchmarks by process. A general template for such a chart is illustrated in Figure 1-8.

This chart lists key business processes in the left column and best-practice companies that are monitored on a regular basis across the top. In each cell it identifies the performance for that process in three time periods: last year, today, and three years from now. This assessment is relative using the scale at the bottom of the page, but it helps to demonstrate change and causes a continuous look at other companies. This approach is well suited for use with a small set of companies that establish a strategic alliance around benchmarking.

BENCHMARKING PROCESS MEASURES

As Dr. Joseph Juran once said: "If you don't measure it, you don't manage it." Process measures are essential to benchmarking. Consider the following questions about any proposed process measure:

- Is it quantifiable?
- How is it measurable?
- What is the measurement precision?
- Where is it auditable?
- When the process changes, how does the measure change?

A good process measure would allow repeatable analyses to take place. Select measures that are true indicators of performance and can be compared across processes. A family of measures is a set of measures that, taken together, provide a broad picture of the process. For instance: quality, cost, and cycle time are the basic set of measures for a process. Using a generally accepted set of measures is much better than using company-specific measures that may not translate into any company's measurement system. Quantify any subjective areas by using rating scales.

Strategic Benchmark Record

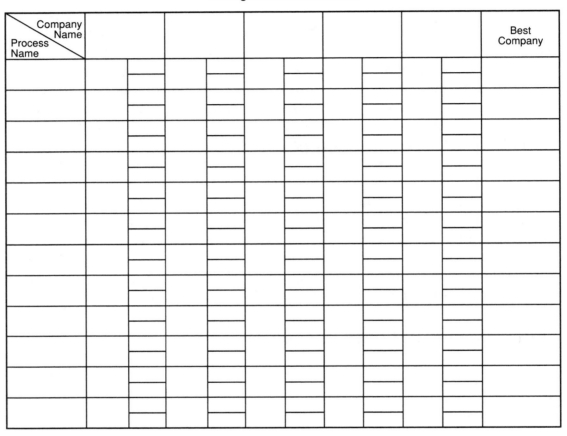

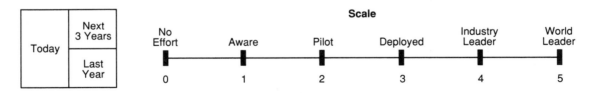

Figure 1-8. Strategic Benchmark Record

Business measures should show the overall performance of the business while process measures should illustrate the contribution of the process to the business.

Examples of business measures include:

Profitability — return on net assets
Financial soundness — debt-equity ratio
Market position — market share
Customer loyalty — customer satisfaction
Productivity — revenue per employee
Flexibility — time to market for new products
Quality — warranty as a percent of sales

Examples of process measures include:

Productivity — transactions per person
Accuracy — error rate
Responsiveness — time interval
Speed — cycle time
Product stability — engineering change orders per month
Process financial contribution — value-to-cost ratio
Product availability — fill rate
Product quality — first-pass yield
Asset utilization — turns ratio
Dependability — variance to commitment
Capacity — volume managed
Service — on-time delivery

In measuring a process, the initial measurement establishes a baseline — a snapshot that tells how well the process is performing at a given point in time. The *baseline* serves as a foundation for the measurement of future improvements. A second measure, called *entitlement*, is the best that can be achieved by the effective use of current resources to eliminate defects or improve cycle time. A *benchmark* indicates the best-in-class performance for a truly optimized process. The relative relationships among these measures is illustrated in Figure 1-9.

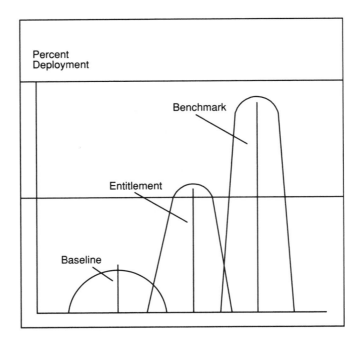

Figure 1-9. Continuous Improvement

BENCHMARKING STUDY PLAN

It is important to have a clear benchmarking study objective for a team to be successful. This is the first element of a benchmarking study plan and perhaps the most important. A guideline that Signetics developed for their benchmarking objective is that it must be SMART:

- **S**pecific
- **M**easurable
- **A**chievable
- **R**ealistic
- **T**ime framed

After the objective has been decided and approved there are other considerations that need to be made regarding the conduct of a benchmarking study.

- Who will conduct the research?
- Who are the beneficiaries (process owners or stakeholders) of the study?
- How many companies and locations need to be considered?

- Are there any particular companies that must be included?
- How is "best" company to be defined?
- How is "best" practice to be defined?
- Are there any particular consultants who would be especially helpful on this project?
- What is the funding available for travel and consulting expenses?

Other elements of the benchmarking study plan are described in Part III under the topic "Creating a Process Benchmarking Procedure."

USING SECONDARY RESEARCH TO MAXIMIZE PROJECT SUCCESS

Secondary research is the primary tool of competitive intelligence; however, it can also provide shortcuts for benchmarking projects. Section 7, "Finding Benchmarking Information Through Secondary Research," provides a detailed look into the use of secondary research methods for benchmarking. The power of secondary research is great. To illustrate how much information has been disclosed in the public domain, APQC performed a study of internal assessment systems based on sources available without seeking direct contact with the organizations. The results of this study are included as Section 8, "Assessing Quality Maturity: Applying Baldrige, Deming, and ISO 9000 Criteria for Internal Assessment." Using secondary research can complement benchmarking by providing knowledge of open-source information about a target benchmarking partner prior to the site visit. This knowledge will help to focus the time available during the site visit on areas that have not been previously disclosed. However, the observation of the power of secondary research is not a blanket endorsement. Much of the information in the public domain either is dated or is public relations "fluff" rather than substantive information about business processes. Any substantive information will need to be verified during a site visit. Getting to the substance of the process requires the direct contact of benchmarking.

NONDISCLOSURE AGREEMENTS

In general it is not wise to seek or receive information that another company considers confidential or proprietary. It is the policy of Xerox that confidential information is not to be disclosed outside the company, and confidential information of others is not to be received by Xerox personnel unless there is a sufficient and compelling business need for doing so. Xerox requires the advance approval of the vice president of the business area receiving the information and the responsible officer-level individual who represents the line management of the business area that is disclosing the information.

A nondisclosure agreement is an agreement between two companies that one company will provide and the other will receive information that is considered to be either confidential or proprietary to the disclosing company. In exchange for the right of disclosure to this information, the receiving company agrees to protect that information from further voluntary or inadvertent disclosure for a specified period of time. To be effective, this agreement needs to be signed by officers of both the providing and receiving companies. The specific items that must be contained in a nondisclosure agreement include:

- Identification of the parties
- Effective date of the agreement
- Date of the disclosure
- Identification of the specific information that is to be protected
- Specific term of the agreement
- Signature, name, title, and date signed by an officer from each organization that is party to the agreement

Your company's legal department should, of course, be consulted on how to create the nondisclosure agreement.

DEVELOPING SURVEYS, QUESTIONNAIRES, AND INTERVIEW GUIDES

Surveys for benchmarking may be delivered by mail, telephone, or in person at interviews or focus groups. In creating and choosing the survey mechanism it is important to know your objectives and the information you seek to collect. The basic approach for all of these survey methods is to:

- Design the questions
- Choose the sample
- Implement the survey
- Follow up to maximize the response rates
- Analyze the results
- Prepare the report

When preparing the questions, keep the respondent in mind—what do you expect the respondent to know to answer your question? Some things to avoid include:

- Vague or overprecise wording
- Double negatives and embedded questions
- Hypothetical questions
- Questions that imply bias
- Overlapping categories
- Abbreviations
- Questions that are too personal or too demanding

Several types of questions can be used:

- Open-ended: may have any possible response
- Closed-ended question with ranked or scaled, forced-response choices
- Closed-ended question with forced or multiple, unranked response choices
- Partially closed-ended: responses are not ranked and have a blank line for "other"

Remember to test your questionnaire in a real-world environment to determine whether a respondent is capable of answering the question and whether there are any reasons why the respondent would decline to answer the question.

An interview guide is a set of questions prepared for a face-to-face interview in a focus group or site visit. Face-to-face communications have some advantages over surveys and questionnaires. The initial agenda is established by the set of questions that define the benchmark study. This should have been received by the partner company several days prior to the benchmark visit. Some of the elements of an interview guide include:

- Opening statement — introduction, purpose of the interview, why the individual was selected for the interview
- Summary of information known about the company
- List of questions to ask — be prepared to explain the relevance of a question
- Prepare a set of your own answers to the questions to share with respondent

During the interview, there are opportunities to probe for material deeper than the surface question. Remember the general guideline for conducting any interview is to LISTEN:

- Look interested
- Inquire with questions
- Stay on target
- Test for understanding
- Evaluate the message
- Neutralize your emotions

After completing the interview, the team should get together for a synthesis session. These are discussions to clarify and consolidate the results of a particular interview. The steps in a synthesis session include the following:

Step 1: Interviewers read over their notes to refresh their memories and impressions of the interview.

Step 2: Beginning with the first section of the interview, interviewers should identify major issues, concerns, strengths, weaknesses, and opportunities that they noted in the comments of the interviewees.

Step 3: Going round-robin, the interviewers should share one observation at a time for that first interview section. These observations should be recorded on flipcharts.

Step 4: After all the major observations are made, the team should create a final list of observations for that section of the interview.

Step 5: Repeat steps 2 through 4 for each section of the interview.

Step 6: When all sections of the interview have been covered, then the team reviews all of the summary points to ensure that they describe the findings of the group.

Step 7: The set of observations are then prepared as a trip report.

DATA ANALYSIS METHODS FOR BENCHMARKING

Before describing the method for developing a "Z" chart, let's consider the basic concept behind the chart. In the upper part of Figure 1-10, there are two different ways that change is measured. The abrupt vertical increase in performance over time comes from an innovative breakthrough improvement in the process. The slower, more gradual change comes from exercising a continuous improvement process that increases the process performance through a series of small incremental steps. Each time an innovative breakthrough occurs, the process is considered to have a new standard of performance; however, this is not true of the continuous improvements. This is because the continuous improvements are barely perceivable to the customer, while the breakthroughs represent visible, customer-perceived improvements.

The lower graph in Figure 1-10 shows company A's historical improvement attained up to the point of the benchmarking study. The vertical line represents the magnitude of the current advantage of company B, the benchmarking partner. This line is projected forward to the milestone date when company A will achieve parity with the benchmark; however, the benchmark performance level is also advanced according to company B's rate of improvement. The new performance goal for this projection must include both the current magnitude of the benchmark gap, and also the amount of company B's continuous improvement trend over that time. This illustration demonstrates that continuous improvement is not enough. (Note: This same phenomenon occurs when customer expectations rise as a result of having them exceeded, thereby creating a new requirement to improve.) Breakthrough change must occur if this company is to obtain parity.

Benchmark data is often displayed in sets indicating the performance of several companies for a specific process measure at a particular point in time (see Figure 1-11).

In this illustration the performance of the company conducting the benchmarking study is at the center and the other companies are grouped around. This quickly illustrates that there is a gap in the degree of performance for this metric. However, to project to the future, we need to translate this graphic into a time domain. Observe the set of three graphics of the "Z" chart in Figure 1-12.

The top graph plots the best-in-class performance level and trend line compared with the current performance of your company. Notice that the difference in the vertical axis is the current benchmark gap.

The middle chart projects from the current time to a future point at which your company will achieve parity with the current benchmark performance. This is plotted by projecting from the current performance level using the

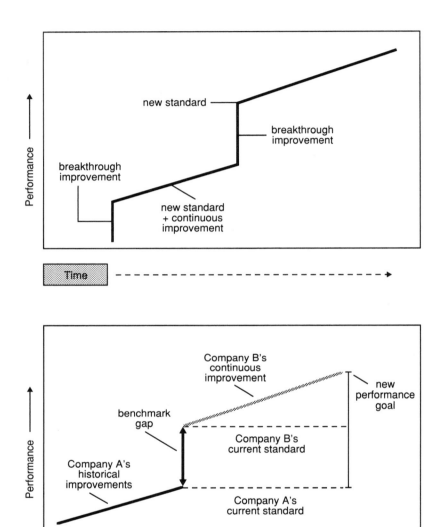

Figure 1-10. Change Mechanisms

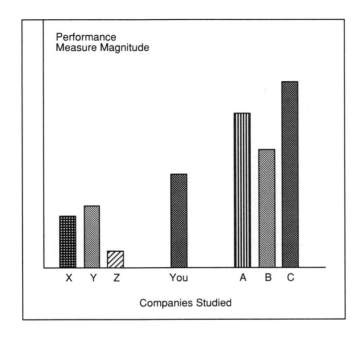

Figure 1-11. Performance Measure Analysis

historical trend of the best-in-class company on the chart. However, this projection is faulty — it assumes that the benchmarked company had no further improvement opportunity.

The bottom chart illustrates a different story, similar to the example above. The improvement rate that your company needs must be faster than the improvement rate of the benchmarked company in order to achieve parity and attain leadership.

This example illustrates the need to carefully select business process goals. Benchmarks can be used to determine the direction of a goal, the magnitude of a goal, and the relative priority for resource allocation when faced with several processes that need improvement.

Goals should be based on the factual data of the best performance observed. Realistic goals should:

- Be based on the proven performance of a benchmarking partner
- Incorporate the benchmarking partner's improvement trends for projection
- Be achievable by adapting best practices to increase performance

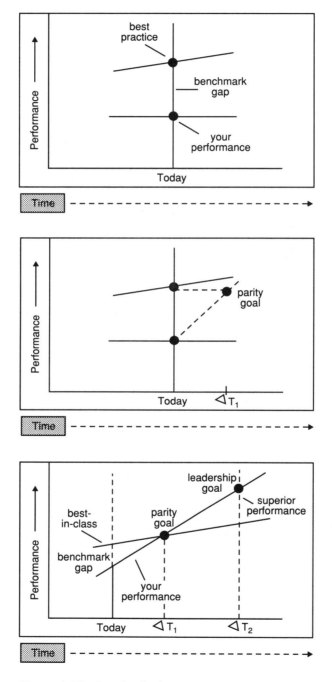

Figure 1-12. Gap Analysis

However, a company cannot become the new benchmark for a process just by doing what the current benchmark company has done in the past. Thus, breakthrough performance is required to get out of this predicament. One new concept that has been discussed is business reengineering for such breakthrough change. This concept is introduced in Section 6, "Comparing Process Models for Benchmarking."

ACTION PLANNING AND TRACKING

To manage change using the three-level strategic change model introduced at the beginning of this section, two plans are required. The first plan is an action plan that records the business situation, objectives, goals, and strategy as developed between senior management and middle management (see Figure 1-13). The second plan is an implementation plan that records the specific steps that will be taken to achieve each of the strategies presented in the action plan as agreed on by the middle managers and the implementation teams (see Figure 1-14). The implementation plan is also used to record the progress of the implementation team. These forms are illustrated on the following pages.

The action plan describes the action to be taken to make the improvement identified in the gap analysis. The form summarizes the study results and identifies the objective of the project. The short-term goal, perhaps parity with the current benchmark, is identified along with a longer-term goal. Each strategy to achieve the objective is identified along with its target and milestones. The strategy elements roughly correspond to the enablers identified during the benchmarking study.

An implementation plan is constructed for each strategy listed on the action plan. This implementation plan is used to monitor the scheduled progress of the implementation teams. This chart is used as a Gantt chart for project scheduling and may be implemented in software on a personal computer.

Benchmarking Action Plan

Process: _____
_____

Critical Success Factor: _____
_____

Process Owner: _____ Date: _____

Summary of Study Results

Objective	**Goals** Short-term
Benchmark Company: _____ Date Observed: _____ Level: _____ Rate: ____	Long-term
Strategy (owner)	**Targets and Milestones**

Source: Gregory H. Watson, *The Benchmarking Workbook* (Cambridge, Mass.: Productivity Press, 1992), p. 93.

Figure 1-13. Benchmarking Action Plan

Benchmarking Implementation Plan

Process: _____

Process Owner: _____ Date: _____

Team Members: _____

_____

Strategy Statement: _____

_____

Activity	Owner	Schedule/Milestones						Performance	
		Month	Month	Month	Month	Month	Month	Target	Actual

Source: Gregory H. Watson, *The Benchmarking Workbook* (Cambridge, Mass.: Productivity Press, 1992), p. 98.

Figure 1-14. Benchmarking Implementation Plan

Part III
Building a
Benchmarking Organization

INTRODUCTION

Benchmarking is a journey rather than a destination. It is not a one-time measurement and analysis, but a continuous practice. To be fully effective, benchmarks must be kept current, and "best-in-class" designations must be regularly reviewed. If benchmarking is to become a permanent feature of an organization's strategic planning system, then an infrastructure must be developed to sustain benchmarking activities. Such an infrastructure would include:

- An organization that coordinates benchmarking activities
- A documented set of procedures and administrative guidelines for benchmarking
- Position descriptions and role models for involved individuals
- Information management to coordinate benchmarking projects
- Project documentation guidelines and benchmarking resource files
- Opportunities for networking with other benchmarking professionals

This section of the guide proposes alternatives for establishing a benchmarking program office, department, or project team within an organization. Since this information must apply to a wide variety of organization types and structures, options are presented for managing benchmarking. This approach allows readers to make appropriate selections from a menu of choices rather than being served a benchmarking "blue-plate special."

DEVELOPING A BENCHMARKING ORGANIZATION

The fundamental issue to be resolved is what will be the focus of benchmarking projects. This issue will serve as a driver for the number of full-time staff members and also for the resources required to support benchmarking. In order to develop an organization that can meet the needs of its customers, it is first necessary to establish the scope of the customer's requirements.

One way to categorize benchmarking projects is by the resources that are necessary to support the project. There are three client levels for process benchmarking projects: senior management, middle management, and grass-roots level.

- *Strategic studies* are conducted for internal clients who seek broad results — typically senior managers who want to gain insights for company-wide change issues. A small professional team with long-term continuity may be required to perform these strategic studies on behalf of senior management. Since these projects tend to support far-reaching or organizationwide change initiatives, these projects conceivably could last for years. Strategic process studies that span multiple internal organizations need the same degree of coordination and management as strategic change projects.
- *Competitive studies* are usually conducted by market research groups to support product development efforts. These studies may branch into process benchmarking whenever management wants to know "what is behind a competitor's performance." These studies can also be conducted by a small group of people — typically a research librarian supported by the market research staff. These studies may lead to strategic benchmarking studies if the competition becomes aggressive enough in process improvement.
- At the *grass-roots level* of an organization, process benchmarking has the widest range of potential applications. These studies tend to look at end-user processes in the organization and may integrate benchmarking activities with total quality team efforts for continuous improvement.

What approach should an organization take to benchmarking: strategic, competitive, or grass roots? Should a hybrid that combines these approaches be considered? One *Fortune* 50 company dedicated its benchmarking effort for years to the strategic level and managed with only four individuals to conduct a multiyear, multinational, cross-industry study. At the other extreme, Xerox is known to have developed a network of more than 300 benchmarkers who study over 400 benchmarked processes.

Other companies have combined benchmarking with market research and focus on the strategic and competitive issues, leaving the operational issues to their individual entities. As a yardstick for resource consideration, one company discovered that the number of individuals who needed in-depth training in benchmarking to support grass-roots level process benchmarking was less than one percent of the population of the employees for that business segment. The remaining employees received only orientation-level training. One added benefit of grass-roots level studies is that the participants are also part of the process team. Thus, it is not necessary to have a full-time study facilitator, particularly if the team leader is also the process owner. This type of benchmarking is most effective when performed by process teams that are empowered to implement change.

Functional management and process-owner involvement and support are crucial to the success and coordination of these studies.

The specific staffing levels required to support benchmarking will also depend upon support levels required by the benchmarking procedures as well as support available from internal researchers, external consultants, and the available formal and informal networks (both internal and external to the organization).

CREATING A PROCESS BENCHMARKING PROCEDURE

A procedure is a formal, internal document that describes the agreed-upon company policy and process steps required to accomplish a particular objective. Some companies have found it helpful to document their benchmarking process as a quality procedure. Such documentation specifies the purpose, charter, or mission of the organization's benchmarking activity, the organizational structure, a definition of the organization-accepted benchmarking model, the resources and training that support the effort, and administrative guidelines for conducting the studies. The following policy items should be included in a benchmarking procedure:

- Responsibilities for managerial supervision of benchmarking activities
- Roles and responsibilities for individuals involved in benchmarking including position descriptions for members of the program office

- Identification of benchmarking coordinators or facilitators with organizations that support the benchmarking activities
- Policy statements for handling incoming benchmarking or information survey requests
- Level-of-approval authority for release of closely held information
- Requirements for nondisclosure statements
- Reporting requirements for tracking the progress of benchmarking studies
- Specification for benchmarking documentation and filing procedures for the final results of a benchmarking study

Two additional tools could also be included in the procedure. One is a matrix that identifies process owners to contact for referral of external information requests. The second tool is a specification for a standard benchmarking study plan that could include information such as:

- Process name and owner
- Short description of the process including process measures and a flowchart
- Rationale for what is to be benchmarked
- Vision for potential process improvements
- Planned approach to the study, including the extent of internal and external benchmarking
- Team member roles, responsibilities, and time commitment
- Project milestones and projected schedule

Formal, written procedures provide a standard approach for conducting benchmarking studies. This benefits the entire organization, since informal studies often do not capture the required information and are usually not distributed to other groups that share a common interest in the process. A procedure or guideline of this type is usually fewer than 35 pages and is reviewed for improvement on an annual basis. The issuing authority for this document is the senior officer in the organization who oversees the benchmarking activity.

DEVELOPING POSITION DESCRIPTIONS FOR BENCHMARKING PERSONNEL

There are seven individual and team roles and four job positions that should be filled in a successful benchmarking program. These include the roles of executive champion, project sponsor, process owner, process stakeholder, project facilitator, team leader, and team members as well as the support positions of benchmarking manager, benchmarking professional, research manager, and information specialist. These roles are not mutually exclusive. For instance, the executive champion may serve as a project manager and process owner for a particular study and then become a process stakeholder in another study. The benchmarking professional may serve as a project facilitator or team member for a benchmarking study. Descriptions of each of these individual roles and their basic responsibilities are provided on the following pages.

Individual and Team Roles

Executive Champion: This role serves as the senior management advocate for process benchmarking. Specific activities may include encouraging the integration of benchmark data into strategic planning, facilitating the establishment of common performance metrics for the entire organization, promoting benchmarking activities to other members of the senior management team, recognizing teams and individuals for their efforts, and serving as the visible senior manager for communicating about benchmarking to the entire organization.

Project Sponsor: The benchmarking project sponsor is often the process owner or the functional manager of the process owner. The sponsor often initiates the benchmarking effort. The sponsor communicates with the team leader and helps to remove internal obstacles that may occur to block the progress of the benchmarking project. The sponsor has the power to make decisions regarding the project and maintains communication with the process stakeholders to coordinate cross-functional issues. The project sponsor is responsible for reviewing progress of the project team and for assessing the findings of the benchmarking team.

Ultimately, the project sponsor is the individual who the team needs to convince that their recommendations should be implemented. The project sponsor is the resource provider for the benchmarking project.

Process Owner: The process owner is the individual who has decision-making control and authority over the particular process that is the subject of the project team. The process owner may also be the sponsor of the project. This individual knows, from management's perspective, where problems and opportunities for improvement exist within the current process. The process owner must participate in the project as either a member of the team or as a member of a management review committee that provides oversight to the team. The process owner is a primary player in the benchmarking effort and should be the most visible management representative for any study that is conducted in his or her functional area.

Process Stakeholder: Process stakeholders are representatives of other internal processes who have either customer or supplier relationships with the process that is the subject of the study. These processes may be potentially affected by any changes in the subject process and, therefore, need to remain informed of the study progress. The process stakeholders provide an external channel of communication to the organization as a whole. They monitor the progress of the study by attending the project review meetings that are periodically held by the process owner.

Project Facilitator: This role is usually held by the benchmarking professional assigned to the project. He or she coaches, facilitates and instructs the team members as they progress through the benchmarking process. The facilitator is the team's owner of the benchmarking process; he or she ensures that the team proceeds effectively. While the facilitator may have content knowledge, his or her role'is to support the team leader, and complement that person as the "content" leader. The facilitator is a gatekeeper who will notice that the team is not functioning properly, needs training, or is unbalanced in terms of individual participation. The facilitator will provide just-in-time training as the team develops a need for more expertise. The facilitator will also interface with the outside consultant and ensure that the team's relationship with external resources is cost-effective. If the facilitator is indeed a professional member of the benchmarking program office, he or she may also coordinate the visits to other organizations and communicate the team's progress and results to the rest of the organization.

Team Leader: The team leader may also be the process owner, project facilitator, or project sponsor. The team leader manages the project resources (consulting expenses, travel budget, etc.) and negotiates with the appropriate managers for financial support. He or she communicates with the process owner and management team, and ensures that the process stakeholders are as actively involved as the scope of the project requires. The team leader also oversees the administration of project logistics, meetings, and issues periodic progress reports to all interested parties.

Team Members: Members are appointed to form the project team based upon their ability to contribute to the study. Members are selected based upon their subject-matter expertise, analytical ability, capability to represent key organizational viewpoints, and willingness to commit the time and effort to serve on the team. Team members are expected to share their expertise and knowledge with the team, encourage the mutual exchange of ideas, convey information back to their own organization, and seek the best possible solutions to meet the study objective. Project teams function well with four to seven members. Teams with more than nine members have difficulty in making progress in their projects, unless they can be divided into subteams that can tackle significant aspects of the project.

Benchmarking Staff Positions

While there are six job classifications that may be used to staff a benchmarking program office (manager, trainer, secretary, research manager, information specialist, and member of the professional staff), the secretary and trainer positions are not unique to benchmarking and can use generic position descriptions. The remaining four positions do require some unique qualifications. Some small organizations will not require both the benchmarking manager and benchmarking professional positions and may consider merging these two into a single position. Likewise, small business will not typically need the manager of research with a supporting staff of information specialists. This is a service that could be obtained on a contract basis. If a choice is made to contract for information searches, it is important that the information service understand the type of data that is required to support benchmarking and that the benchmarking professional understands how to set up on-line information searches. To assist in the preparation of position descriptions, the qualifications for these positions are described below.

Benchmarking Manager: The benchmarking manager typically reports in to the quality organization, the planning organization, or the market research organization. This manager has the cost center management and budgeting responsibility. In addition, he or she is responsible for:

- Defining the organization-specific approach to process benchmarking
- Developing the resources necessary to support benchmarking
- Training the organization in benchmarking
- Assuring that benchmarking protocol and agreed-upon conduct are followed

- Monitoring and encouraging the progress of benchmarking projects
- Facilitating the development of an implementation plan
- Recognizing the contribution of benchmarking teams
- Promoting the application of benchmarking throughout the organization

The benchmarking manager should be selected from among the ranks of the company's respected internal managers. The individual who serves as benchmarking manager will be exposed to the entire breadth and depth of the organization. This position is a good growth path for the development of a future potential senior manager. The individual who is selected for this position needs the following skills, experiences, and characteristics:

- Management experience from one of the organization's key business processes
- Strong communication skills and a broad internal network of contacts
- Practical understanding gained as a practitioner of total quality management
- An ability to see and understand the strategic business perspective
- Good problem-solving skills and command of the basic quality tools
- Strong sense of ethical action and a managerial presence that conveys trust
- Demonstrated responsible resource administration

Benchmarking Professional: The benchmarking professional is responsible for providing project analysis and internal consulting to teams about the benchmarking process. This role offers the services the grass-roots level needs for education, facilitation, application, and promotion of benchmarking. The professional participates as a team member in key benchmarking projects, and facilitates those projects whose scope does not require direct support. The benchmarking professional is expected to keep current with the latest developments in benchmarking and to develop and maintain an external network of contacts among potential external benchmarking partner organizations and consulting organizations. He or she is also the organization's conscience and enforcer of the Benchmarking Code of Conduct. In addition, the benchmarking professional is responsible for:

- Facilitating the documentation of internal processes and evaluation of internal benchmarks
- Evaluating the process documentation to develop generic terms and performance measures that can apply outside of the organization's specific business area

- Developing the key word thesaurus and monitoring the execution of the preliminary secondary research
- Conducting analysis of internal and secondary data that target specific organizations as potential benchmarking partners
- Developing the questionnaire, survey form, or interview guide that is used to guide the project investigation
- Drafting all formal communication with external organizations about benchmarking projects
- Coordinating the logistics of site visits to external organizations
- Facilitating the analysis of site-visit information to develop gap analysis and making specific recommendations for improvement activities
- Ensuring that benchmarking status reports, final reports, and project briefings are included in the organization's benchmarking data repository

To succeed, the benchmarking professional needs to develop credibility with the grass-roots organization by demonstrating professionalism in both conduct and the application of tools. This is not an entry-level position. It requires business experience and understanding of industry practices. It also requires acceptance by the grass-roots organization. A junior-level position may be created in some companies as an entry-level position for new hire graduates with a master's degree in business administration who also have solid experience from another company. This entry-level person could be mentored by an experienced benchmarker in the process of benchmarking and in an orientation to the organization's political and cultural dimensions. Specific skills, experience, and characteristics of a benchmarking professional include:

- Professional experience in one of the organization's key process areas
- Strong statistical and analytical skills with experience in developing questionnaires
- Ability to communicate with the operational level of the organization
- Practical experience in total quality management or continuous quality improvement teams
- Ability to prepare cost estimates and manage contractual agreements with external suppliers of benchmarking support
- Interviewing and presentation skills
- Strong organizational and planning skills
- Ability to use computer systems for central data base applications, electronic mail, and basic personal computer applications

- Tact, diplomacy, and the ability to negotiate a consensus path when faced with team member or external partner personality issues
- Experience in using and staffing of the information service function

Research Manager: In some large organizations, it may be necessary to have an individual serve as coordinator of secondary research activities and administrator of benchmarking data bases and information repositories. The responsibilities of this position include:

- Designing, developing, and implementing information systems, resources, and procedures to support the internal benchmarking efforts, including both information data base and a repository of benchmarking project reports
- Providing on-demand research services to internal customers using external data bases
- Designing and developing an organization-specific thesaurus of process identifiers, terms, and performance measures to form an internal catalog system that supports secondary research for key-word searches
- Maintaining a file of successful key-word searches for all key business processes
- Identifying and acquiring new information sources for the benchmarking technical library
- Managing the use of external suppliers of information services
- Monitoring industry activities for organizational key business processes by providing a news-clipping service bulletin board for each identified key business process
- Maintaining a file of all benchmarking nondisclosure agreements
- Maintaining the specific handling procedures as requested by benchmarking partners for their restricted distribution information

The specific skills required for the research manager position include extensive data base searching experience and previous management experience in the field of information services. Good communication and customer service skills are also essential. The research manager will also manage the organization's budget for purchase of library research materials and data base search services. A final skill is the ability to effectively contribute to the discussion of substantive business issues with the process owners and benchmarking team members. This individual is a peer with the benchmarking professional.

Information Specialist: The information specialist supports the research manager in large companies. This position has the primary responsibility of acquiring and providing high-quality information to support benchmarking activities. Specific responsibilities include:

- Providing rapid response to information inquiries through commercial data base searches
- Editing, synthesizing, and focusing search outcomes prior to sending them to the customer
- Assisting in the development, cataloging, and administration of the benchmarking technical library materials
- Scanning literature to identify articles, books, periodicals, and reports that should be acquired for the benchmarking technical library
- Providing systems administration for the benchmarking electronic bulletin board
- Establishing and managing all key business-process clipping services

The skills required of an information specialist include extensive data base search capability, with the use of DIALOG® a must. The ability to work within tight deadlines and discuss business issues also contribute to the success of this position. As with the research manager, good interviewing, communication, and customer-service skills are important.

These roles and responsibilities need to be clarified for every organization that embarks on a formal benchmarking effort and establishes a benchmarking program office. Those roles and positions that are chosen for an organization benchmarking effort may be recorded in the process benchmarking procedure as well as in position descriptions filed with the organization's personnel staff.

COORDINATING AND MANAGING STUDIES ACROSS ORGANIZATIONS

In large multinational corporations it is difficult to coordinate benchmarking activities.

To conduct cost-effective benchmarking, it is important not to duplicate research efforts. One way to eliminate duplication is to coordinate benchmarking study efforts through a central data base or status reporting system. Such a system provides overall project management support and facilitates communication among professional benchmarkers who are distributed across the organization. This application is well suited for an information technology project;

however, manual files could achieve the same result. Even small organizations can benefit from a file of this sort since it can also be used as a tickler file when benchmarking information needs to be recalibrated. The information in this type of file might include:

- File of active, inactive, and completed benchmarking projects, including abstracts of all reports and reference to the location of the project file that includes the benchmarking project plan, interim status reports, briefing overheads or slides, and the final report
- Study directory with a file of planned benchmarking projects and current progress status reports for ongoing benchmarking projects, including contact names and locations
- Directory of individuals who have received training in benchmarking
- Directory of external services approved or recommended for use in benchmarking studies
- Listing of process owners to contact for response to external benchmarking inquiries
- Companywide file of executed third-party nondisclosure agreements with the scope and extent of the agreement specified
- Electronic bulletin board to serve as an open forum for discussion of benchmarking techniques, announcements of new benchmarking projects, clarification of current study issues, consolidation of study efforts, and the clipping service information for key business processes
- Bibliography of information received from external sources about benchmarking
- Electronic newsletter to announce symposia, training, and networking events

This registry of benchmarking information could be used to support company efforts for both internal and external benchmarking studies. This information should be cross-referenced and accessed through an information retrieval system that is maintained by the benchmarking technical library.

DOCUMENTING BENCHMARKING RECORDS AND STUDIES

One tool necessary to support such an organizationwide benchmarking information system is the project abstract. This is the recorded form of the "best practice" identified in the study. In addition, this needs to be correlated with the definition of current key business processes to permit comparison of current, measured performance with the collected set of "best-in-class" information. The basic format for this "best practice" is the process template described in Part II. In addition to the information described in the process template, the following information could be included:

- Key words to identify the process, performance measures, and functional area
- Indicators of performance level and comparisons with American industry, worldwide industry, and world-class best performance
- Trend indicators to show where progress is being made relative to external standards and internal improvements
- Statement of the background situation that leads to measuring this process as well as the current goals, objectives, and strategies for improvement of this process

NETWORKING AMONG BENCHMARKING ORGANIZATIONS

A network is a decentralized organization of independent participants who develop a degree of interdependence and share a coherent set of values and interests. Networks connect people with people and link ideas with resources. Networking occurs when one person with a need contacts another person with a resource. Thus, networking is a connection among peers.

Networks have three qualities:

- *Segmentation:* Networks are composed of autonomous individuals who are independently self-sufficient.
- *Decentralization:* Networks have fluidly changing leadership roles and are connected by horizontal, rather than vertical linkages.
- *Unification by values:* Networks are connected by an ideological bond of shared values, goals, interests, and purposes.

Networks have a loose structure and are composed of unpredictable entities that participate in this organizational structure to develop its own identity. A network seems to be intangible because so much of the meaning of a network is established by member relationships: the linkages, communication, friendship, and trust that breathe life into the network. By this definition, a network is about human interaction and cooperation. In a sense, benchmarking is about networking.

A network of benchmarkers can share at several levels. Individuals who are beginning their benchmarking journey have a set of introductory-level concerns and issues:

- What is benchmarking?
- Who is doing it?
- Where can I learn about it?
- What can I read?
- Where do I get started?
- What are the pitfalls?
- Where can I find success stories?

Individuals who have been conducting benchmarking projects for some time have a deeper level of concerns and issues:

- What policies should guide our benchmarking efforts?
- What guidelines exist for intercompany sharing?
- What guidelines exist for ethical considerations in information exchange?
- Where are the best sources of information?
- Where can I meet with other individuals who conduct benchmarking projects?
- Where can I discover who is the appropriate contact for a particular benchmarking project?

Section 2
Industry's Benchmarking Practices: Executive Summary of a Survey by the International Benchmarking Clearinghouse

- Overview
- Purpose
- Survey Method and Respondents
- Participating Companies
- Major Finding 1: Increase in Benchmarking
- Major Finding 2: Perceptions of Benchmarking
- Major Finding 3: Leading Companies Are Benchmarking
- Major Finding 4: User Experience Levels in Benchmarking
- Major Finding 5: Benchmarking Studies
- Major Finding 6: Benchmarking Requests
- Major Finding 7: Factors Encouraging Benchmarking
- Major Finding 8: Steps in the Benchmarking Process
- Major Finding 9: Benchmarking Training and the Team Approach
- Major Finding 10: Factors Contributing to Successful Benchmarking
- Major Finding 11: Factors When Benchmarking Is Unsuccessful
- Major Finding 12: Valuable Products and Services to Benchmarkers
- Summary and Conclusion

OVERVIEW

Benchmarking is a process in which companies target key improvement areas within their firms, identify and study best practices by others in these areas, and implement new processes and systems to enhance their own productivity and quality. Many leading companies are finding that in today's globally competitive market, you benchmark and improve — or you don't survive. Benchmarking, a continuous improvement process within the total quality management (TQM) revolution, enables companies to look outside their own walls in the ongoing search for excellence.

PURPOSE

Despite the paramount importance of benchmarking, little data exist pertaining to the state of benchmarking in American industry. As a step toward developing a collective knowledge base of benchmarking practices, the International Benchmarking Clearinghouse (IBC) administered a survey in October of 1991 to its members and other companies. Following brief descriptions of the survey methodology and respondents, an executive summary of major findings is provided.

SURVEY METHOD AND RESPONDENTS

Method — The IBC surveyed 87 IBC "Design Steering Committee" member organizations. A total of 76 surveys were returned (a response rate of 87 percent). In some cases, more than one survey was received from the same company, but from different business units. Only one survey per business unit within a company was allowed. In addition, responses from associations were deleted from the analysis sample. Based on these criteria, 68 responses remained and represent the present sample.

Respondents — Of the survey participants, 67 percent represent management, 18 percent senior staff, and 15 percent senior management. The majority (58 percent) of respondents have held their current titles from one to three years, while 22 percent report less than one year in their position. Most have roles related to the leadership, coordination, development, or implementation of benchmarking efforts within their organizations. In the survey, 56 percent answered for their entire company or corporation, 38 percent for their entire group or strategic business unit, and 6 percent for one facility or unit within a group.

Most major industries are included in the present sample. Industries most strongly represented are (1) electronics/computers, (2) energy, (3) utilities, (4) insurance, (5) financial services, and (6) aerospace/defense. Eighty-eight percent of the respondents view their organizations as the leaders or among the leaders, in most markets (see Major Finding 3). To protect confidentiality, data for individual companies are not reported. A list of participating companies follows.

SURVEY PARTICIPANTS

AMP Incorporated
AT&T
Alcoa
Alliant Techsystems Inc.
Allstate Insurance Co.
American Express Company
Baxter Healthcare Corp.
Boise Cascade Corporation
Browning-Ferris Industries Inc.
Chevron Corporation
Compaq Computer Corporation
Deere & Company
Digital Equipment Corporation
DuPont
Electronic Data Systems
Enron Corporation
Harris Corporation
Helene Curtis Incorporated
Honeywell Inc.
Hughes Aircraft Company
IBM Corporation
I.T.T. Defense
Intel Corporation
International Paper

Lanter Company
Lifeline Systems, Inc.
Litton Data Systems
Marriott Corporation
MasterCard International
Metropolitan Life
Motorola, Inc.
NASA
NCR Corporation
NYNEX
National Semiconductor Corporation
The New England
Northern Telecom
Olin Corporation
Pacific Bell
Pacific Gas & Electric Co.
Pennzoil Company
Phillips Petroleum Co.
Powell Industries, Inc.
Preston Trucking
The Prudential Insurance Company
    of America
SERVISTAR Corporation
Shell

The Southland Corporation
TRW Incorporated
Tandem Computers Incorporated
Tenneco Corporation
Texas Instruments Incorporated
The Timken Company

UNISYS
USAA
U.S. Customs Service
U.S. West Communications
Westinghouse Corporation
Xerox

MAJOR FINDING 1

Increase in Benchmarking

There has been a dramatic increase in the amount of benchmarking in the past year, and this trend is expected to continue.

Although some companies, such as Xerox, began benchmarking as early as 1980, there has been a dramatic increase in benchmarking in the recent past. Compared with one year ago, more than 75 percent of the survey sample indicate that the amount of benchmarking in their firms has increased more or significantly more (Figure 2-1). During the next five years, 96 percent of these organizations expect more or significantly more benchmarking (Figure 2-2). Clearly, the data suggest that benchmarking is on the rise within the present sample of organizations.

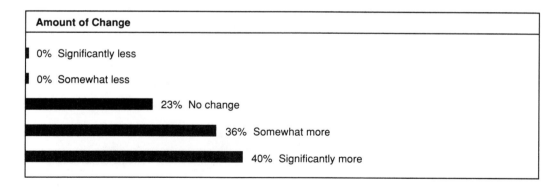

Amount of Change

- 0% Significantly less
- 0% Somewhat less
- 23% No change
- 36% Somewhat more
- 40% Significantly more

Figure 2-1. Increase in Benchmarking in Last Year (N = 47)

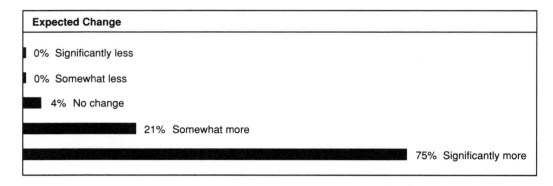

Figure 2-2. Increase in Benchmarking Next Five Years (N = 48)

MAJOR FINDING 2

Perceptions of Benchmarking

Benchmarking is a necessary tool for survival, but most firms don't know how to do it.

Table 2-1 reports respondents' levels of agreement with several statements regarding benchmarking. Surprisingly, 95 percent agree that most companies do not know how to benchmark, and 89 percent believe that success can occur only if top management is committed. Seventy-nine percent agree that companies will have to benchmark to survive. Is benchmarking here to stay? Only a little more than one-fourth (28 percent) think that benchmarking is a fad, while the majority (57 percent) disagree.

Additionally, nearly 50 percent agree that benchmarking has already improved their products and services, while only 15 percent disagree (data not shown). Can everyone afford to benefit from benchmarking? Only 8 percent be-

Table 2-1. Perceptions of Benchmarking (N = 66)

Statements	Somewhat/ Strongly Agree	Somewhat/ Strongly Disagree
Companies will have to benchmark to survive	79%	8%
Most companies don't know how to benchmark	95%	2%
Benchmarking is a fad	28%	57%
Benchmarking succeeds only if top management is committed	89%	6%
Small companies cannot afford the cost of benchmarking	8%	79%

Rating Scale: 1 = strongly disagree; 2 = somewhat disagree; 3 = neither agree nor disagree; 4 = somewhat agree; 5 = strongly agree.

lieve that small companies cannot afford the cost of benchmarking, while 79 percent disagree.

MAJOR FINDING 3

Leading Companies Are Benchmarking

Leading companies from most industries are benchmarking, and 90 percent of the benchmarkers have an active total quality management (TQM) process under way.

Seventy-four percent are using the Malcolm Baldrige National Quality Award criteria for self-assessment, even though 51 percent plan to apply for the award in the next five years.

Benchmarking is not limited to any one type of industry. Virtually every major type of industry is represented in the present sample of benchmarkers, including aerospace/defense, communications, chemicals, electronics/computers, energy, financial services, health care, insurance, and utilities.

As the saying goes, "the best keep getting better"; 88 percent of the respondents view their organizations as the leaders or among the leaders in most markets (Figure 2-3). As is often the case, it is the leading-edge companies that pave the way for the rest to follow. Perhaps benchmarking has been chosen as a method to maintain the competitive lead that many of these firms enjoy.

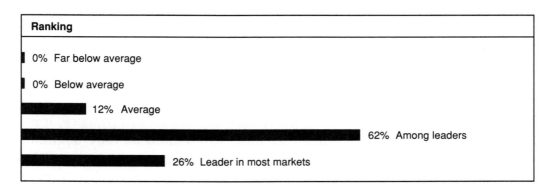

Ranking

- 0% Far below average
- 0% Below average
- 12% Average
- 62% Among leaders
- 26% Leader in most markets

Figure 2-3. Ranking of Company's Competitive Position (N = 66)

While benchmarking is not limited to any one type of industry, there is an apparent relationship between organizations using TQM and those that are benchmarking. It is not surprising that 90 percent of the present sample indicated that their organizations have an active TQM process under way (Figure 2-4).

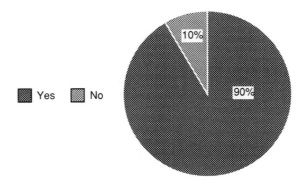

Figure 2-4. Use of Active TQM Process (N = 68)

While benchmarking is included in the criteria for the Malcolm Baldrige National Quality Award (MBNQA), only 28 percent of the present sample have applied (Figure 2-5). Seventy-four percent of respondents indicate that their company is currently using the MBNQA criteria for self-assessment (Figure 2-6). Only 51 percent plan to apply for the MBNQA in the next five years (Figure 2-7).

MAJOR FINDING 4

User Experience Levels in Benchmarking

The majority of firms consider themselves to be beginner or novice users of process (83 percent) and competitive (70 percent) benchmarking.

Because benchmarking is a relatively new organizational practice, it is not surprising that 83 percent consider their organizations to be only beginner or novice users of process benchmarking (Figure 2-8). A lesser percentage (70 percent) consider their firms to be beginner or novice competitive benchmarkers (Figure 2-9). There is a slightly higher percentage of intermediate or advanced users of competitive benchmarking. Perhaps this finding is attributable to the more mature practice of competitive intelligence gathering, a predecessor to the more recent benchmarking. Overall it is clear that benchmarkers consider themselves to be relatively inexperienced.

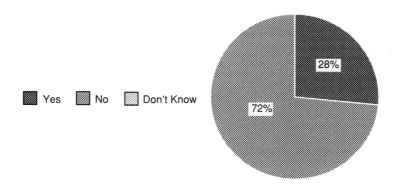

Figure 2-5. Past Application for the MBNQA (N = 68)

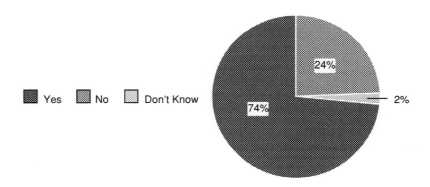

Figure 2-6. Using MBNQA Self-Assessment Criteria (N = 66)

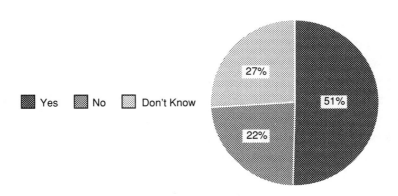

Figure 2-7. Plan to Apply for the MBNQA (N = 67)

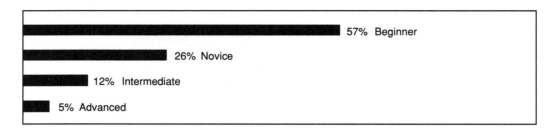

Figure 2-8. User Experience in Process Benchmarking (N = 65)

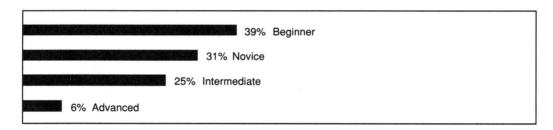

Figure 2-9. User Experience in Competitive Benchmarking (N = 65)

MAJOR FINDING 5

Benchmarking Studies

Nearly half of the companies (47 percent) have been conducting benchmarking studies for less than two years, while 20 percent have been benchmarking for more than five years.

Over half (51 percent) have conducted 2 to 5 process benchmarking studies, while only 15 percent have done more than 20.

Given the low experience level of most benchmarkers in our sample, it is not surprising that not all of them have conducted benchmarking studies. As shown in Figure 2-10, however, 72 percent report that process or competitive benchmarking studies have been conducted in their organizations.

Consistent with the low experience level of most benchmarkers in our sample, of the 49 organizations that have conducted studies, nearly half (47 percent) have been doing so for less than two years (Figure 2-11). Further, about half (51 percent) have conducted only two to five process benchmarking studies, and only 15 percent have done more than 20 studies (Figure 2-12). A slightly greater number of competitive studies have been conducted, with 21

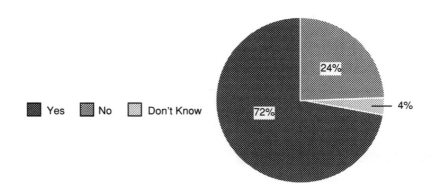

Figure 2-10. Have Conducted Process or Competitive Benchmarking Studies (N = 68)

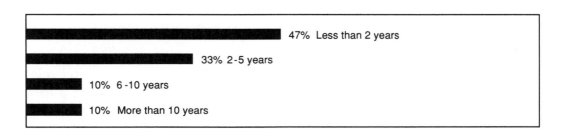

Figure 2-11. Years Conducting Benchmarking Studies (N = 49)

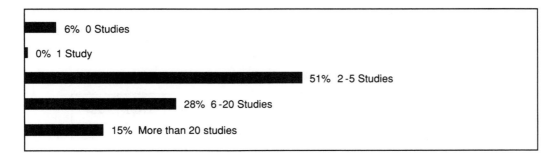

Figure 2-12. Number of Process Studies Conducted (N = 47)

percent in the more than 20 range, and 44 percent in the 2 to 5 category (Figure 2-13).

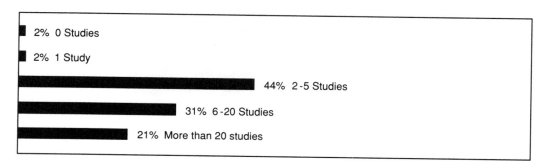

Figure 2-13. Number of Competitive Studies Conducted (N = 48)

MAJOR FINDING 6

Benchmarking Requests

As benchmarking increases, so does the number of benchmarking-related requests companies receive. Yet, 82 percent indicate they do not have a formal process for responding to requests.

Companies may expect to receive more benchmarking requests as benchmarking practices increase. Table 2-2 reports the percentage of benchmarkers that are receiving a variety of benchmarking requests. The most prevalent requests are for phone interviews, with 47 percent of the present sample receiving more than five of these. A sizable percentage of organizations also report having received five or more requests for questionnaires (33 percent), site visits (31 percent), and written material about processes (30 percent). In addition, 41 percent report having received at least one "How to Benchmark" request.

Table 2-2. Benchmarking Requests in the Past Year (N = 65)

Type of Request	0	1-5	6-10	11-20	20+
Written material about processes	26%	43%	12%	3%	15%
Telephone interviews	16%	38%	16%	13%	18%
Site visits	27%	42%	9%	5%	17%
Questionnaires	28%	39%	13%	8%	12%
"How to Benchmark"	59%	26%	0%	5%	10%

Considering the number of requests that many benchmarkers are receiving, it is surprising that so few have a formal process for responding to these requests (Figure 2-14). Perhaps the development of necessary policies and procedures to handle benchmarking requests has not yet caught up with the demand.

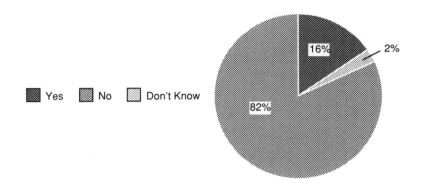

Figure 2-14. Have Regular Process for Responding to Requests (N = 66)

MAJOR FINDING 7

Factors Encouraging Benchmarking

Top management commitment, the desire for better customer service, financial performance, product development cycle, and delivery time are driving factors encouraging firms to benchmark.

Ninety-three percent of those doing benchmarking studies report at least some top-management support for the process.

Survey respondents were asked to rate the importance of factors encouraging benchmarking in their companies. Not surprisingly, top-management commitment emerges as the number-one factor, with 82 percent rating this factor as being of great or very great importance (Table 2-3). Customer service level and financial performance also ranked at the top of the list. Two processes — product development cycle and product delivery time — also surfaced as driving factors of benchmarking.

While management support was cited as an important factor encouraging benchmarking, lack of top-management support was found to be a factor contributing to unsuccessful benchmarking studies and implementations. As reported in Figure 2-15, more than 90 percent of the sample that have conducted

Table 2-3. Importance of Factors Encouraging Benchmarking (N = 65)

	Mean	Great/Very Great Importance	Little/Very Little Importance
Top management commitment	4.4	83%	3%
Customer service level	4.1	82%	2%
Financial performance	3.8	65%	8%
Product development cycle	3.8	68%	14%
Product delivery time	3.7	65%	16%

Rating Scale: 1 = very little importance; 2 = little importance; 3 = some importance; 4 = great importance; 5 = very great importance

benchmarking studies report at least some management support and acceptance of benchmarking. Forty-one percent report great or very great top management support and acceptance. This support appears to be a necessary (though insufficient) condition to the success of benchmarking.

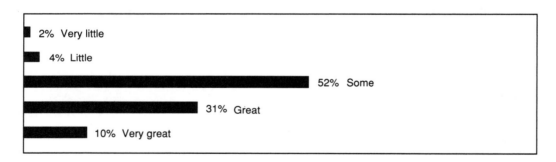

Figure 2-15. Top Management Support and Acceptance of Benchmarking (N = 48)

MAJOR FINDING 8

Steps in the Benchmarking Process

More than 80 percent report using a benchmarking process model, while the specific number and nature of steps varies greatly among benchmarkers.

Of the firms that have conducted benchmarking studies, 81 percent are using some form of benchmarking process; 20 percent report they are using the Xerox method, or a variation thereof. As might be expected, the specific number and nature of steps used to conduct benchmarking studies varies greatly among firms. Differences in terminology and levels of analysis are likely to account for this. It is clear that there is no one "correct" model of benchmarking.

Despite differences in benchmarking models, common denominators do exist. Typical steps used to benchmark include: (1) Preparation; (2) Research; (3) Selecting Partners; (4) Collecting and Sharing Information; and (5) Analyzing, Adapting, and Improving. Substeps of these major phases of benchmarking are provided in Figure 2-16. (See full survey report and Section 6, "Comparing Process Models for Benchmarking," for a detailed description.)

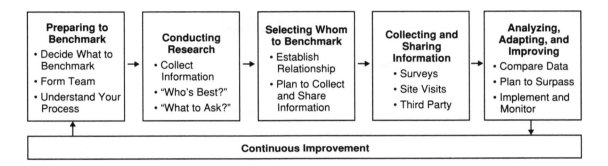

Figure 2-16. Common Steps in Benchmarking Models

MAJOR FINDING 9

Benchmarking Training and the Team Approach

Ninety-four percent report using a team approach to benchmarking. This suggests that a team approach to benchmark training is appropriate.

The most important skill for benchmarking study participants is process analysis, followed by "soft" skills such as communications and team building.

Ninety-four percent of the organizations surveyed that have conducted benchmarking studies are using a team approach (Figure 2-17). This indicates benchmarking is not an individual effort. Some of these companies use dedicated facilitators to assist the teams while others use their natural teamwork process for self-facilitation. Benchmarking training is suggested for intact study teams and may provide a good approach for aligning the efforts of the individual members when a professional benchmarking facilitator is not available.

In our respondents' view, process analysis is the most important skill for benchmarking study participants, with 98 percent rating this as important or very important on a five-point scale (Table 2-4). This is not surprising, since

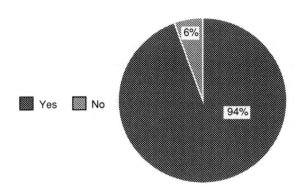

Figure 2-17. Use Team Approach in Benchmarking (N = 47)

"Understanding Your Process" is the most important factor to a successful study (discussed below in Major Finding 10). Other important skills are of a "softer" nature and include: (1) Communications, (2) Team Building, (3) Interpersonal Relations, and (4) Conducting Meetings. This finding, combined with the frequent use of a team approach, suggests that team-oriented benchmarking training for both technical and nontechnical skills may be desirable.

Table 2-4. Importance of Skills for Benchmarking Study Participants (N = 48)

	Mean	Great/Very Great Importance	Little/Very Little Importance
Process analysis	4.6	98%	0%
Communications	4.5	94%	0%
Team building	4.2	88%	0%
Interpersonal relations	4.2	88%	0%
Conducting meetings	3.8	62%	2%

Rating Scale: 1 = very little importance; 2 = little importance; 3 = some importance; 4 = great importance; 5 = very great importance

MAJOR FINDING 10

Factors Contributing to Successful Benchmarking

Overwhelmingly, the key factors in a successful benchmarking study are "understanding your process" and "process-owner involvement."

Survey participants were asked to rate several factors with respect to their importance in a successful benchmarking study. Overwhelmingly, 98 percent rated "understanding your process" and "process-owner involvement" as being of great or very great importance to a successful study (Table 2-5). Other important factors included: (1) Results Implemented; (2) Selection of Benchmark Targets; and (3) Initiated by Process Owner. As a group, these factors represent some of the keys to a successful benchmarking study.

Table 2-5. Factors Contributing to Successful Benchmarking (N = 45)

	Mean	Great/Very Great Importance	Little/Very Little Importance
Understanding your process	4.8	98%	0%
Process-owner involvement	4.6	98%	0%
Results implemented	4.3	84%	2%
Selection of benchmark targets	4.2	87%	0%
Initiated by process owner	4.2	89%	4%

Rating Scale: 1 = very little importance; 2 = little importance; 3 = some importance; 4 = great importance; 5 = very great importance

MAJOR FINDING 11

Factors When Benchmarking Is Unsuccessful

Poor planning, lack of process-owner involvement, no top-management support, and insufficient skills are cited as the most frequent reasons a benchmarking study is not successful.

Unfortunately, not all benchmarking studies and implementations are successful in creating improvement in an organization. Firms participating in the survey were asked to rate the extent that several factors contribute to unsuccessful studies and implementations. "Poor planning" and "No top-management support" rose to the top of this list (Table 2-6). Additional factors included: (1) No Process-Owner Involvement, (2) Insufficient Benchmarking Skills, and (3) Low Priority. The limited agreement as to what factors are most important when benchmarking is unsuccessful may suggest that these factors vary greatly among organizations, while strengths are more common.

Table 2-6. Factors When Benchmarking Is Unsuccessful (N = 42)

	Mean	Great/Very Great Extent	Little/Very Little Extent
Poor planning	3.8	65%	15%
No top-management support	3.8	61%	28%
No process-owner involvement	3.6	61%	24%
Insufficient skills	3.5	56%	22%
Low priority	3.1	36%	24%

Rating Scale: 1 = very little extent; 2 = little extent; 3 = some extent; 4 = great extent; 5 = very great extent

MAJOR FINDING 12

Valuable Products and Services to Benchmakers

When asked what they needed from a benchmarking clearinghouse, the top responses were: (1) A compilation of best practices by process, (2) Names of company contacts, (3) A data base of performance measures, (4) Abstracts of benchmark studies, and (5) A "how-to" reference manual.

Organizations were asked to what extent various products and services of a benchmarking clearinghouse would be of value to their companies. Based upon the mean ratings, the following five products and services ranked at the top of the list: (1) Best practices by process, (2) Names of company contacts, (3) Performance measures data base, (4) Abstracts of benchmarking studies, and (5) A "how-to" reference manual (Table 2-7). Subsequent surveys confirm the importance of these products and services.

Table 2-7. Valuable Products and Services to Benchmarkers (N = 68)

	Mean	Great/Very Great Extent	Little/Very Little Extent
"Best Practices" by process	4.6	93%	2%
Names of contacts	4.5	90%	0%
Performance measures data base	4.3	86%	0%
Benchmark study abstracts	4.1	75%	5%
"How to" reference manual	4.0	74%	6%

Rating Scale: 1 = very little extent; 2 = little extent; 3 = some extent; 4 = great extent; 5 = very great extent

SUMMARY AND CONCLUSION

Benchmarking activity has increased dramatically since 1990, and many of the nation's leading organizations are doing it. A large percentage of firms believe that benchmarking is a necessary tool for survival, and that many organizations do not yet know how to benchmark. Most are beginner or novice users of benchmarking and have conducted few benchmarking studies. There is still time to be a leader in benchmarking! Successful benchmarking requires top-management commitment, conscientious planning, training, and a thorough understanding of one's own processes to be benchmarked.

Section 3
Applying Moral and Legal Considerations to Benchmarking Protocol

"One may use his competitor's secret process if he discovers the process by reverse engineering applied to the finished product; one may use a competitor's process if he discovers it by his own independent research; but one may not avoid these labors by taking the process from the discoverer without his permission at a time when he is taking reasonable precautions to maintain its secrecy. To obtain knowledge of a process without spending the time and money to discover it independently is improper unless the holder voluntarily discloses it or fails to take reasonable precautions to ensure its secrecy."

E.I. duPont de Nemours & Co. v. Christopher, 401 U.S. 967 (1971)

INTRODUCTION

Morality and legality are two dimensions of behavioral choice. "Moral" implies right or wrong behavior or judgments based upon the prevailing standard that is applied by conforming to the actual behavior of a specific community at large. Thus, moral behavior implies standards of behavior that are relative to a particular community. "Legal" implies right or wrong behavior or judgments that are based upon established formal standards or rules of law. Thus, legal behavior implies an absolute standard that is set and enforced by a regulatory or judicial body.

In the case of benchmarking, the accepted moral standard is the professional Code of Conduct jointly approved by the Strategic Planning Institute's Council on Benchmarking and the American Productivity & Quality Center's International Benchmarking Clearinghouse (see Appendix A). This code summarizes the protocol of benchmarking — the set of conventions prescribing correct etiquette and procedures to be used in conducting benchmarking studies. In addition to this prescribed moral behavior, there are legal expectations that define the specific boundaries of acceptable behavior among benchmarking partner companies.[1]

While moral imperatives do not have the force of legal obligation, it should be noted that the repercussions of immoral behavior are just as strong as illegal behavior. Consider the case of Xerox when benchmarking was introduced. When Xerox first disclosed the practice of benchmarking to the public, journalists likened it to "industrial espionage." Xerox was depicted as a "spy master," and the whole practice was put into question. This was an incorrect perception, since successful benchmarking is not based upon either immoral or illegal behavior. A moral or a legal departure from acceptable behavior can have serious consequences for a company in terms of both its internal morale and its external reputation. Immoral behavior can cripple the morale of employees by causing divisiveness among employees of principle. From an external perspective, immoral behavior causes a company's reputation to be diminished. Thus, moral behavior is of significant importance to a company's image.

MORAL ASPECTS OF INFORMATION ACQUISITION

Moral considerations are particularly important in the conduct of the intercompany relationships necessary for benchmarking. A study by Richard F. Beltramini indicated the need for making such moral considerations visible. Beltramini studied a sample of 500 individuals who were involved in competitive information acquisition in blue-chip U.S. corporations. He stated: "The findings of this exploratory investigation indicate that those individuals involved in competitive information acquisition are willing to misrepresent themselves and/or take liberties beyond the limitations of ethical corporate policy."[2] Beltramini's investigation also indicated that the majority of those interviewed believed that other companies were less ethical in their practices. This study gives us reason for concern about our sense of moral behavior.

It is particularly noteworthy that there is a fundamental distinction between competitive intelligence and benchmarking. That fundamental distinction has to do with the degree of openness with which an organization pursues its study. The fact that a company is the target of a competitive intelligence study is itself a confidential matter. In benchmarking, however, the objective is to develop an open sharing of information directly with the target company. In this environment, the atmosphere of "industrial espionage" is eliminated because the conduct of the investigation itself is not a secret to the other party. There are still many areas, however, where proper considerations must be made for the conduct of the study.

Concern about the use of information acquired during benchmarking and its subsequent use prompted the development of the Benchmarking Code of Conduct (see Appendix A). The underlying principle of the code is the Golden Rule — do unto others as you would have them do unto you. Whenever moral questions occur during an information search, it is appropriate to apply a basic rule: avoid any practice or conduct that would cause public embarrassment to your company or yourself if it were revealed in the *Wall Street Journal*. If you have any doubt, see your organization's legal counsel for advice.

LEGAL ASPECTS OF INFORMATION ACQUISITION

There are three legal considerations of which benchmarkers should be aware: antitrust law, laws on industrial espionage, and restrictive clauses related to intellectual property.

Conditions for Antitrust Violation

Many of the considerations about the legal aspects of intercompany relationships exist because of concern about antitrust legislation. Antitrust acts are federal and state statutes that are intended to protect trade and commerce from unlawful restraints, price discrimination, price fixing, and monopolies. The principal antitrust acts are the Sherman Act (1890), Clayton Act (1914), Federal Trade Commission Act (1914), and the Robinson-Patman Act (1936).

Restraints of trade are contracts or associations that tend to or are designed to eliminate or stifle competition, cause a monopoly, artificially maintain prices, or otherwise obstruct the course of trade and commerce compared with the movement of natural economic forces. In antitrust legislation, legal action is caused by unreasonable restraints in trade. These include business and commercial transactions that tend to restrict production, affect prices, or otherwise control a market to the detriment of purchasers or consumers. These acts are made unreasonable because their specific intention is to create a limit on the open market by controlling pricing or product distribution.

In any situation where two or more businesses get together to discuss "business," there should be concern about creating a "combination in restraint of trade." Combinations in restraint of trade are agreements or understandings between two or more persons in the form of an association whose purpose is to unduly restrict competition, monopolize trade, or control production, price, or distribution without the necessary statutory authority.

The legal consideration for determining the legality of restraints on trade weighs all factors of the case including the history of the restraint, the evil believed to exist, the reason for the particular activity and its business purpose. For instance, publicly identifying "worst-in-class" could be construed as a "vendor boycott" and could lead to the imposition of criminal penalties both against a company and the individual who makes the claim. To constitute a crime under the Sherman Antitrust Act, the defendant's conduct must result in an unreasonable restraint of interstate commerce. It is left to a jury to determine whether the actions of individuals or companies are sufficient causes of unreasonable restraint on interstate commerce. The jury evaluates both the economic conditions of the industry and the effect on competition of the company's action to determine the sufficiency of the cause of action for creating an unreasonable restraint on interstate commerce.

Clearly, any circumstances where competitive businesses meet to discuss "improvement" activities are open for interpretation in the light of these statutes. Most companies would not consider violating these statutes in the spirit of the law; however, it is possible to violate the letter of the law by exchanging pricing, sales, cost, results or future market strategy information with competitors. It is important that due diligence be exercised by all participants in these activities to prevent the occurrence of situations that could imply the conditions described above. As in all legal matters, it is best to advise corporate lawyers of the situation involved in information sharing and to allow them to review any documents or agreements that govern the conditions for sharing.

The Legal Boundaries of Competitive Intelligence

Common law has provided a rule for interpreting the boundaries of competitive intelligence — an important legal ruling, in the case of *E.I. duPont de Nemours & Co. v. Christopher* regarding the interpretation of Texas state law for protecting the intellectual property of inventors from improper appropriation. In brief, Christopher operated a private aircraft for hire and was hired to fly over DuPont property and photograph a new plant under construction. Upon discovery, DuPont sued for the name of the individual or company who hired Christopher. Christopher refused to divulge this information. The legal issue was how far a company could go to obtain information about other companies. In the final ruling by the Federal Court of Appeals, several important judicial rules were established. The first is contained in the opening quotation to this section, which implies that reverse engineering and independent research are both acceptable to understand the moves of competitors.

In their ruling the court noted that "commercial privacy must be protected from espionage which could not have been reasonably anticipated or prevented." They also stated:

Reasonable precautions against predatory eyes we may require, but an impenetrable fortress is an unreasonable requirement, and we are not disposed to burden industrial inventors with such a duty in order to protect the fruits of their efforts. "Improper" will always be a word of many nuances, determined by time, place, and circumstances. We therefore need not proclaim a catalogue of commercial improprieties. Clearly, however, one of its commandments does say "thou shalt not appropriate a trade secret through deviousness under circumstances in which countervailing defenses are not reasonably available."[3]

While this ruling did not provide a clear rule for interpreting reasonable protection or proper circumstances for protection, it did extend the definition that had been previously used — that specific acts of physical trespass needed to occur before an act of espionage could be proven. Christopher was found to have exceeded the limit of prudent observation of a competitor.

Restrictions on Intellectual Property Ownership

A final area where benchmarkers should be aware are the types of restrictions placed on the ownership of intellectual property. These restrictions may be classified into four categories.

These categories cover the areas of ownership, security, information handling, and the extent of the application of restrictions. These areas include such considerations as:

- Ownership: assignment of patent, copyright, trademark, and future commercial rights.
- Security: classification of company material as confidential or proprietary, subject to nondisclosure, and the extent of these bindings required for third-party employees.
- Handling: requirements for exclusivity of relationships, information distribution, and timeliness of notification of the creation of substantive intellectual property.
- Extent of intellectual property: material improvements, inventions, discoveries, ideas, or concepts, which may be made, conceived, suggested, created, or invented in connection with work for a company as a direct employee or third-party contributor.

EXPECTED BEHAVIOR OF BENCHMARKERS AND BENCHMARKING PROTOCOL

In contrast to competitive intelligence, benchmarking is a collaborative effort between participating companies. Sharing information between companies requires a basic understanding of how to conduct the benchmarking study. A basic approach for ethical benchmarking is contained in the following list of practices. These practices form the protocol, or set of conventions, that guides the actions of professional benchmarkers:

1. Know and abide by the *Benchmarking Code of Conduct*.
2. Have basic knowledge of benchmarking and follow a benchmarking process.
3. Prior to initiating contact with potential benchmarking partners, determine what to benchmark, identify key performance variables to study, recognize superior performing companies, and complete a rigorous self-assessment.
4. Develop a questionnaire and interview guide, and be willing to share these in advance if requested.
5. Possess the authority to share and be willing to share information with benchmarking partners.
6. Work through a specific host, and mutually agree on scheduling and meeting arrangements.

When the benchmarking process proceeds to a face-to-face site visit, the following behaviors are encouraged:

- Provide the meeting agenda in advance.
- Be professional, honest, courteous, and prompt.
- Introduce all attendees and explain why they are present.
- Adhere to the agenda.
- Use language that is universal, not one's own jargon.
- Be sure that neither party is sharing proprietary information, unless prior approval has been obtained by both parties from the proper authority.
- Share information about your own process, and, if asked, consider sharing study results.
- Offer to facilitate a future reciprocal visit.
- Conclude meetings and visits on schedule.
- Thank your benchmarking partners for their time and for sharing their process.

BENCHMARKING ETIQUETTE AND ETHICS

In the actions between benchmarking partners, the emphasis is on openness and trust. The following guidelines apply to both partners in a benchmarking encounter:

1. In benchmarking with competitors, establish specific ground rules up front, e.g., "We don't want to talk about things that will give either of us a competitive market advantage, but rather we want to see where we both can share information and learn lessons that will allow us to improve the performance of our internal business processes."
2. Do not ask competitors for sensitive data or cause the benchmarking partner to feel they must provide data to keep the process going.
3. Use an ethical third party to assemble and "blind" competitive data, with inputs from legal counsel, in direct competitor sharing. (Note: When cost is closely linked to price, sharing cost data can be considered to be the same as price sharing.)
4. Benchmarkers should check with legal counsel if any information gathering procedure is in doubt, e.g., before contacting a direct competitor. If uncomfortable, do not proceed or sign a nondisclosure agreement. Instead, you should negotiate the specific terms of a nondisclosure agreement that will satisfy the attorneys from both companies.
5. Any information obtained from a benchmarking partner should be treated as internal, privileged communications. If "confidential" or "proprietary" material is to be exchanged, then a specific agreement should be executed to indicate the content of the material that needs to be protected, the duration of the period of protection, the conditions for permitting access to the material, and the specific handling requirements that are necessary for that material.

TIPS ON BEHAVIORAL ISSUES: DO'S AND DON'TS

As the *DuPont* case indicated, business secrets should not be discovered by improper means. Determining what specific practice is moral or legal may be difficult, so the following tips are provided to help clarify these descriptions. These issues are divided into good, bad, and questionable issues or practices. Another area to consider is the behaviors that can alienate your professional colleagues.

Good Practices

- Using secondary research to locate public documents about the target company
- Purchasing competitive products in the open market and performing reverse engineering
- Conducting market research and customer-satisfaction surveys
- Gathering information at trade shows
- Soliciting other companies directly to share information about targeted processes
- Building a data base of information from company employees who formerly worked for competitors

Bad Practices

- Trespassing upon another company's property with the intent to collect information
- Bribing individuals to act as informants
- Bugging or eavesdropping on another company's privileged or private communications
- Planting agents on another organization's payroll
- Learning, even inadvertently, about a competitor's pricing considerations
- Creating a breach of confidential relationship by a third party (supplier, accountant, lawyer, or consultant)
- Conducting fake job interviews, either as a recruiter or an applicant
- Deliberately misrepresenting your affiliation, company, or identity to obtain information
- Flying over another company's property or using a telephoto lens to obtain information that would otherwise remain "protected"
- Trading in the stock of a company after learning about "material" information that has not been publicly disclosed (insider information) — a violation of the Securities and Exchange Commission regulations
- Requiring participation in a study as a precondition for obtaining business

Questionable Practices

- Recruiting employees from competing companies for the purpose of obtaining information
- Asking questions at a technical meeting without identifying your company and name
- Subscribing to competitors' technical journals or attending user conferences as a private individual to avoid exposing your company affiliation

Things to Look Out for

- Referring to another organization or to their information while visiting a third-party organization
- Giving information in a public forum about a benchmarking partner without the partner's specific permission
- Asking for information that you are not willing to provide
- Initiating contact and setting up a visit without first doing your internal benchmarking "homework"
- Bypassing the designated host of your benchmarking partner to change the agenda or to set up side activities beyond the agreed-upon benchmarking event
- Requesting last-minute changes or additions to the visit agenda

A FINAL ANALYSIS

In the final analysis, each person's own conscience must guide his or her actions. The standard that benchmarking requires is high because it deals with opening an information network that has been traditionally closed in our society. It is clear that benchmarkers should be aware of the circumstances of their information search and question their actions to determine the most appropriate information acquisition strategy that will bear the scrutiny of the public moral and legal requirements. The American Productivity & Quality Center and the Strategic Planning Institute have agreed to follow the Benchmarking Code of Conduct in their benchmarking activities. Please take the time to read, understand, and internalize the code. If you have questions about its meaning, do not hesitate to call either organization to help clarify the meaning of the section that is not understood.

NOTES

1. Leonard Fuld proposes a set of both moral and legal guidelines in his following "Ten Commandments":

    1. Thou shalt not lie when representing thyself.
    2. Thou shalt observe thy company's legal guidelines.
    3. Thou shalt not tape-record a conversation.
    4. Thou shalt not bribe.
    5. Thou shalt not plant eavesdropping devices.
    6. Thou shalt not deliberately mislead anyone in an interview.
    7. Thou shalt neither obtain from nor give price information to thy competitor.
    8. Thou shalt not swap misinformation.
    9. Thou shalt not steal a trade secret (or recruit employees in hopes of learning trade secrets).
    10. Thou shalt not knowingly press someone for information if it may jeopardize that person's job or reputation.

    Leonard M. Fuld, *Monitoring the Competition: Finding Out What's Really Going on Over There*, New York: John Wiley & Sons, 1987, p. 167.
2. Richard F. Beltramini, "Ethics and the Use of Competitive Information Acquisition Strategies," *Journal of Business Ethics*, 5, 1986, pp. 307 - 311.
3. The complete legal citations for this case are: 431 F.2d 1012 (5th Cir.) *reh. and reh. en banc denied* (1970), *cert. denied*, 400 U.S. 1024, *reh. denied*, 401 U.S. 967 (1971).

Section 4
Analyzing the Cost of Benchmarking Studies:
A Model for Comparison

- Introduction and Purpose
- Background Data
- Benchmarking Cost Model
- Total Benchmarking Investment

INTRODUCTION AND PURPOSE

It is difficult to evaluate the potential cost of benchmarking if your company has no experience in this area. As a guide for companies, the American Productivity & Quality Center's International Benchmarking Clearinghouse has created this cost model based on a survey of the members of the Design Steering Committee.* This model is intended to provide a framework for companies to estimate and put into perspective the costs of benchmarking.

The model can be used by beginning benchmarkers to estimate what their investment is likely to be, if they follow standard practices in benchmarking. It can be used by experienced benchmarkers to estimate how their costs compare to others.

Both groups can also be the model to identify costs that might be avoided or minimized by using the Clearinghouse services.

BACKGROUND DATA

The survey of benchmarking practices asked for responses to many questions about benchmarking, including the estimated time and costs to benchmark. Survey responses from over 80 leading American organizations provided data that constitute the basis for this model.

Please note the following:

- Each organization is obviously different. Costs and benefits associated with benchmarking vary considerably from study to study and from company to company. Cost assumptions have been made conservatively, based upon the data.
- Data shown in the model delineates costs only. It does not quantify benefits.
- Companies responding to the survey overwhelmingly indicated the benefits were very significant, with some studies reporting payoffs of more than five times the cost of the study. Returns on investment can take the form of reduced costs, increased sales, customer retention, enhanced

---

* For details on the survey, see the Clearinghouse publication (Benchmarking Survey - Full Report).

market share, or greater customer satisfaction and loyalty. Survey respondents overwhelmingly indicated that they intend to increase their benchmarking efforts.

BENCHMARKING COST MODEL

Companies are involved in many activities related to benchmarking, both in their solicitations of information and in their responses to the requests of other organizations. In the survey of the members of the Design Steering Committee, an attempt was made to quantify the total cost of benchmarking. The results of these survey questions are the basis for the following benchmarking cost model.

The column headed "Survey Average" has information that shows averaged data from the companies that completed the survey, or answered telephone follow-up questions. You can compare your answers with the survey average to provide a rough comparison against other companies that are benchmarking. To make this comparison, answer the following questions by filling in the column headed "Your Company."

If your answers vary considerably from the average, it may be worth exploring what your company does that contributes to the difference, and how that may affect your overall benchmarking efforts.

Responding to Written Material Requests

Questions	Survey Average	Your Company
1. How many requests for written material related to benchmarking does your company get in a year?	6.6	_____
2. What do you estimate is the total handling cost of each written-material request, including postage, salaries, and overhead?	$50.00	_____
3. Multiply the above two answers for your average annual cost of handling written-material requests. (6.6 × $50 = $330.00)	$330.00	_____

Handling Telephone Interviews

Questions	Survey Average	Your Company
4. How many requests for telephone interviews related to benchmarking does your company get in a year?	8.8	_____
5. What do you estimate is the total handling cost of each telephone interview, including tolls, salaries and overhead?	$50.00	_____
6. Multiply the above two answers for your average annual cost of handling telephone interview requests. (8.8 × $50 = $440.00)	$440.00	_____

Completing Questionnaires

Questions	Survey Average	Your Company
7. How many requests for written questionnaires related to benchmarking does your company get in a year?	6.4	_____
8. What do you estimate is the total handling cost of each questionnaire request, including postage, salaries, and overhead?	$60.00	_____
9. Multiply the above two answers for your average annual cost of handling questionnaire requests. (6.4 × $60 = $384.00)	$384.00	_____

Explaining How to Benchmark

Questions	Survey Average	Your Company
10. How many requests for information on how to benchmarking does your company get in a year?	4.0	_____
11. What do you estimate is the total handling cost for each how-to-benchmark request, including postage, salaries, and overhead?	$50.00	_____
12. Multiply the above two answers for your average annual cost of how-to-benchmark requests. (4.0 × $50 = $200.00)	$200.00	_____

Hosting Site Visits

Questions	Survey Average	Your Company
13. How many requests for site visits related to benchmarking does your company get in a year?	7.0	_____
14. A) How many team members participate on an average when hosting a site visit?	5.6	_____
B) How many hours does the team work to negotiate, gain approvals, make presentations, plan visit activities, analyze questionnaires, diagnose and document processes, and host the visiting company? Include average individual time on new team tasks.	32.0	_____
C) How many employee-hours per hosted visit? (5.6 × 32 = 179.2)	179.2	_____
D) What is your hourly overhead rate per person?	$50.00	_____
E) Total cost per visit (14C × 14D or 179.2 × $50 = $8,960.00)	$8,960.00	_____
15. Multiply (13) × (14E) for the total annual cost of hosting visits. (7.0 × $8,960.00 = $62,720.00)	$62,720.00	_____

Processing Benchmarking Studies

Questions	Survey Average	Your Company
16. How many site visits do you include in your average benchmarking study?	3.3	_____
17. How many hours are used for each site visit, including travel both ways?	16.0	_____
18. Multiply the last two answers for travel and visit hours per person. (3.3 × 16 = 52.8)	52.8	_____
19. How many team members participate on an average?	5.6	_____
20. Multiply the previous two answers to get total employee-hours used in travel and visits. (52.8 × 5.6 = 295.7)	295.7	_____
21. How many hours does the team meet to plan, understand its own process, negotiate site visits, analyze gaps and causes, adapt information, sell, implement, and follow through on the implementation of improvements?	104.0	_____
22. Multiply the above hours by the number of team members for a subtotal of hours. (104.0 × 5.6 = 582.4)	582.4	_____
23. Add (20) + (22) for total employee hours. (295.7 + 582.4 = 878.1)	878.1	_____

Processing Benchmarking Studies (cont.)

Questions	Survey Average	Your Company
24. Multiply the above hours by the hourly salary and overhead rate for your company for the Total Cost of Time. (878.1 × $50 = $43,905.00)	$43,905.00	_____
25. What are your estimated average site visit travel costs per person?	$500.00	_____
26. Multiply the average travel costs by the average number of team members. ($500 × 5.6 = $2,800.00)	$2,800.00	_____
27. Multiply the previous number by the number of site visits per study. ($2,800.00 × 3.3 = $9,240.00)	$9,240.00	_____
28. Add the Total Cost of Time (from question 24) to the previous number to get the total cost of one complete process benchmarking study. ($43,905.00 + $9,240.00 = $53,145.00)	$53,145.00	_____
29. How many process benchmarking studies does your company do in a year?	8.8	_____
30. Multiply the last two answers to get the total annual estimated cost of process benchmarking in a year for your company. (8.8 × $53,145.00 = $467,676.00)	$467,676.00	_____

Competitive Benchmarking Studies

Questions	Survey Average	Your Company
31. How many site visits do you include in your average benchmarking study?	3.3	_____
32. How many hours are used for each site visit, including travel both ways?	16.0	_____
33. Multiply the last two answers for travel and visit hours per person. (3.3 × 16 = 52.8)	52.8	_____
34. How many team members participate on an average?	5.6	_____
35. Multiply the previous two answers to get total employee-hours used in travel and visits. (52.8 × 5.6 = 295.7)	295.7	_____
36. How many hours does each team member work to plan, understand the process, negotiate site visits, prepare questions, identify measures, analyze gaps and causes, adapt information, sell, implement, and follow through on the implementation of improvements?	112.0	_____
37. Multiply the above hours by the number of team members for a subtotal of hours. (112.0 × 5.6 = 627.2)	627.2	_____
38. Add (35) + (37) for total employee	922.9	_____

Competitive Benchmarking Studies (cont.)

Questions	Survey Average	Your Company
39. Multiply the above hours by the hourly salary and overhead rate for your company for the Total Cost of Time. (922.9 × $50 = $46,145.00)	$46,145.00	_____
40. What are your average travel costs per person?	$500.00	_____
41. Multiply the average travel costs by the average number of team members. ($500 × 5.6 = $2,800.00)	$2,800.00	_____
42. Multiply the previous number by the number of site visits per study. ($2,800.00 × 3.3 = $9,240.00)	$9,240.00	_____
43. Add the Total Cost of Time from question 39 to question 42 to get the total cost of one complete competitive benchmarking study. ($46,145.00 + $9,240.00 = $55,385.00)	$55,385.00	_____
44. How many competitive benchmarking studies does your company do in a year?	10.4	_____
45. Multiply the last two answers to get the total annual estimated cost of competitive benchmarking in a year for your company. (10.4 × $55,385.00 = $576,004.00)	$576,004.00	_____

Training

Questions	Survey Average	Your Company
46. How many people are trained how to benchmark each year in your company?	120.00	_____
47. What do you estimate is the total cost to train each employee in benchmarking skills, including time, tuition, and travel?	$1,000.00	_____
48. Multiply the above two answers for your average cost of benchmarking training. (120 × $1,000.00 = $120,000.00)	$120,000.00	_____

Total Benchmarking Cost Each Year

Questions	Survey Average	Your Company
Responding to written-material requests	$330.00	_____
Handling telephone interviews	$440.00	_____
Completing questionnaires	$384.00	_____
Explaining how to benchmark	$200.00	_____
Hosting site visits	$62,720.00	_____
Process benchmarking studies	$467,676.00	_____
Competitive benchmarking studies	$576,004.00	_____
Training	$120,000.00	_____
Total without consulting fees	$1,227,754.00	_____

Consulting

Questions	Your Company
How much do you spend on consulting fees for benchmarking each year in your company? Add any consulting fees to the total above for your total corporate annual benchmarking cost.	_____ _____

TOTAL BENCHMARKING INVESTMENT

The average cost of benchmarking can be calculated by dividing the total number of studies completed (questions 13 and 29: 7.0 + 8.8 = 15.8) into the total annual benchmarking investment ($1,227,754.00). Based on the cost model, the average cost for each study would be $70,111.00.

To see how your costs compare, divide the total annual cost of benchmarking for your company by the number of studies used for your calculations.

According to survey question 49, "What is the full cost of a typical study?" the average benchmark study costs were $67,857.00. This value compares favorably with the model that we have developed.

Section 5
Evaluating Benchmarking Training: A Survey of Training Courses

- Overview
- Types of Training and Development Products to Support Benchmarking
- Training Time Requirements
- Benchmarking Skills Training — Content
- Supplemental Training Activities to Support Benchmarking
- Special Considerations
- Ensuring Success

OVERVIEW

Purpose

Organizations that choose to implement process benchmarking quickly discover the need to train and develop their people to support it. This study summarizes the current status of benchmarking training in organizations that use or offer benchmarking seminars. The following questions will be explored:

- What types of training and development products are needed to support benchmarking?
- How much training time is needed?
- What content and skills do the participants need to learn?
- What supplemental training or activities are needed to support benchmarking?
- Do special considerations need to be accommodated in the training?
- How can training and development ensure the success of a benchmarking initiative?

Research Method

In the fall of 1991, the International Benchmarking Clearinghouse conducted a survey of its membership. Responses were obtained from 76 companies. A subset of 68 companies currently doing benchmarking was created and used for this study. All nonresponses to survey items were deleted from the statistical calculations. More details on the survey population, design, and analysis are contained in Section 2, "Industry's Benchmarking Practices: Executive Summary."

Summary of Survey Findings

The survey produced five major findings for those who are charged with training and development to support benchmarking:

1. The importance of classes and publications to prepare a company to implement benchmarking was clear. Both methods were cited by over 65 percent of survey respondents.

2. A large range of skills was cited as important for benchmark study participants. The top-rated skill was process analysis (4.58 on a five-point scale). It was closely followed by several soft skills: communications, team building, and interpersonal relations. These skills are typically addressed in basic training for Total Quality Management.

3. There was a wide range of responses on just how much training is required to participate in or lead a benchmarking study. Responses ranged from under 4 hours to participate in a study to over 40 hours to lead a study.

4. On the topic of how much training it takes to be a benchmarking trainer, two distinct approaches were presented. Of our respondents, 24.3 percent felt that less than 4 hours of training were needed to be a benchmarking trainer. Conversely, 35 percent felt that more than 40 hours of specialized training were needed.

5. The strongest finding in the entire survey directly affects everyone charged with training to support benchmarking: 93.6 percent of all responding companies use teams to conduct benchmarking studies. Clearly a successful training plan to support benchmarking needs to accommodate teams both in its design and in the actual classroom participation.

TYPES OF TRAINING AND DEVELOPMENT PRODUCTS TO SUPPORT BENCHMARKING

Analysis of the survey results and ongoing discussions with experienced benchmarkers indicate a need for three training and development products to support a benchmarking effort: Benchmarking Presentation to Management, Benchmarking Skills Workshop, and training on How to Manage Benchmarking. Details on the three follow.

Benchmarking Presentation to Management

An overview of what benchmarking is, its potential costs and benefits, and supporting statements from various quality authorities would be presented to corporate leaders. This may take the form of a presentation or senior management dialogue rather than a formal course. The audience should include key members of management whose support is needed for the start of benchmarking efforts. Typical durations of 30 to 90 minutes are cited.

In response to the question, "How important are the following factors in encouraging benchmarking in your company?" the respondents rated top-management commitment highest of 13 choices, 4.37 on a five-point scale. The survey also examined the tools used to prepare a company for benchmarking (see Figure 5-1).

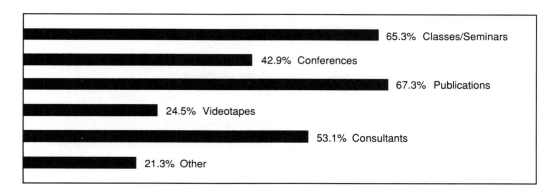

Figure 5-1. Which Education and Training Tools Did You Use to Prepare the Company for Benchmarking?

Most companies report using multiple tools to prepare their employees, with training classes or seminars and publications being the most frequently cited. For a list of publications on benchmarking, please see Section 9, "A Bibliography of Benchmarking Literature." Benchmarking Presentations to Management would be developed and owned by an internal benchmarking champion or a department assigned the responsibility for benchmarking.

Benchmarking Skills Workshop

The second product needed to support benchmarking would be a skills-oriented training program. The programs studied ranged in length from one to three days. Typical of this product offering are instructionally sound, professionally developed courses. These were owned by internal quality, benchmarking, or training departments. Several organizations offer such courses to the public (see Table 5-1.)

Most Clearinghouse members with internal benchmark training programs report having developed their own materials. As the practice of benchmarking becomes more consistently defined, organizations wishing to have internal

Table 5-1. Benchmarking Skills Workshops

Organization	Length	Outline/Agenda
American Management Association (518) 891-0065	2 days	Intro to benchmarking Why benchmarking works Benchmarking process Planning a benchmarking process for your organizations Benchmarking investigation Integration Implementation Getting started
American Productivity & Quality Center (713) 581-4020	2 days	What is benchmarking Benchmarking process Determining what to/not to benchmark Selecting the study Collecting internal data Finding best in class Gathering data from comparison organization Benchmarking interviewing Analyzing data Integrating data Setting goals, objectives, plans Benchmarking documentation
American Society for Quality Control (800) 248-1946	2 days	Competitive benchmarking defined Motivation, planning Case studies Comparing your performance Closing the gap Communicating findings Implementing benchmarking
AT&T Benchmarking Group (908) 580-6120	2 days	Benchmarking benefits and overview 9-step model What to benchmark Identify variables and collect data Measure self Best in class Compare, develop plans, implement, monitor Recalibrate Incorporating benchmarking in your organization
Competitive Dynamics, Inc. (310) 397-6055	1 day	Introduction to benchmarking Prerequisites for benchmarking 8-step process Getting started Next steps

These listings represent ongoing, public programs offered as of July 31, 1992. Inclusion on this table in no way indicates endorsement or approval by the American Productivity & Quality Center.

Organization	Length	Outline/Agenda
The Manufacturing Institute (800) 345-8016	2 days	Structure and conduct benchmarking investigations Identify which functions to benchmark Determine best-in-class companies Pinpoint the key performance variables to measure Collect, analyze, and compare benchmarking data Implement action plans to achieve significant benefits
The Quality Network (214) 380-0300	2 days	What should be benchmarked first? How do we select benchmark teams? What are some pitfalls to avoid? How long should projects take? What about cross-functional processes? How do we get management committed? How do we measure improvement? What resources are required?
Strategic Planning Institute (617) 491-9200	2 days (members only)	The benchmarking process Organizing and gathering information Assimilating and taking action Implementing a benchmarking program
Verity Consulting (213) 389-9700	2 days	Benchmarking defined Benchmarking's role in strategic planning History of benchmarking Case studies 8 steps of benchmarking Benchmarking exercises Benchmarking and total quality
Washington Researchers (202) 333-3499	1 day	Framework for benchmarking Benchmarking defined The process. Completing benchmarking project Making benchmarking permanent Decisions using benchmarking
Washington State University Institute for Quality and Productivity (509) 335-3530	2 days	Benchmarking and charge management Identification of benchmark alternatives From benchmarking to performance improvement Managing benchmarking for performance
George Washington University (800) 424-9773	2 days	What is benchmarking? Prerequisites for benchmarking Benefits of benchmarking Role of benchmarking in TQM Types of benchmarking The process. Implementation action plan

programs will be able to adapt "stock" programs from training suppliers to their needs. This offers the opportunity to reduce some of the costs currently associated with starting a benchmarking effort.

How to Manage Benchmarking

The third training and development product seen as essential for a successful benchmarking initiative is How to Manage Benchmarking. The content would include how to start, support, and sustain benchmarking activities. The limited audience size of this product (typically only one person per organizational unit need attend) means that such training is likely to be offered only by the few centers of benchmarking knowledge.

TRAINING TIME REQUIREMENTS

How much training is needed to provide benchmarking skills? The survey broke this topic down into four segments:

- Participate in a benchmarking study
- Lead a benchmarking study
- Conduct benchmarking training
- Manage benchmarking

A high percentage of survey respondents indicated that four hours (or less) of training was adequate to conduct or lead a benchmarking study. This response may have been skewed by the availability of experienced benchmarking facilitators in many of the companies surveyed. The presence of a professional benchmarking facilitator would tend to reduce the need for training. When a benchmarking study is initiated or led by others, participants would seem to need a minimum of about a half-day training event, based on the data in Figure 5-2a.

The survey results were unclear regarding the minimum number of classroom training hours needed to lead a benchmarking study. As shown in Figure 5-2b, the responses show no discernible trend or prevailing opinion.

The inconsistent results in Figure 5-2b may be explained, in part, by the wide range of content cited as essential for benchmarking. A further discussion of this possibility follows in the "Benchmarking Skills Training – Content" section of this study.

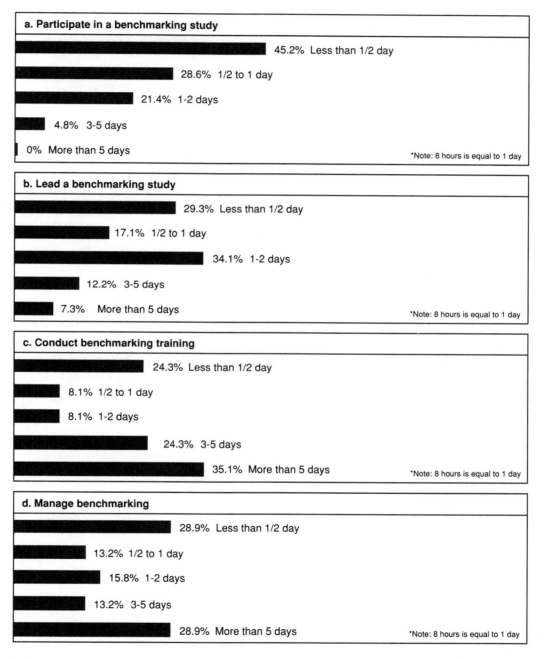

a. Participate in a benchmarking study

45.2% Less than 1/2 day

28.6% 1/2 to 1 day

21.4% 1-2 days

4.8% 3-5 days

0% More than 5 days

*Note: 8 hours is equal to 1 day

b. Lead a benchmarking study

29.3% Less than 1/2 day

17.1% 1/2 to 1 day

34.1% 1-2 days

12.2% 3-5 days

7.3% More than 5 days

*Note: 8 hours is equal to 1 day

c. Conduct benchmarking training

24.3% Less than 1/2 day

8.1% 1/2 to 1 day

8.1% 1-2 days

24.3% 3-5 days

35.1% More than 5 days

*Note: 8 hours is equal to 1 day

d. Manage benchmarking

28.9% Less than 1/2 day

13.2% 1/2 to 1 day

15.8% 1-2 days

13.2% 3-5 days

28.9% More than 5 days

*Note: 8 hours is equal to 1 day

Figure 5-2. In Your Company, What is the Minimum Number of Hours of Classroom Benchmarking Training Necessary for an Individual to Perform the Following Functions?

Another survey item sought to determine the minimum amount of training needed to conduct benchmarking training. The results show two widely divergent opinions (Figure 5-2c).

The survey did not specify whether the training content was on benchmarking or generic instructor skills or both. Please see a related discussion on this point in the "Special Considerations" section of this study.

The minimum amount of training needed to manage benchmarking was examined in the next survey item. As seen in Figure 5-2d, a bipolar response pattern makes clear interpretation difficult.

The wide range of benchmarking experience among respondents may play a role in the distribution of opinions on this topic. An additional confounding factor is the wide range of business entities that constitute benchmarking organizations.

BENCHMARKING SKILLS TRAINING — CONTENT

Organizations that are just initiating their benchmarking efforts are tempted to ask for a content outline of an "ideal" benchmarking course. Each organization will have different training needs based upon maturity of their total quality management (TQM) process. The content of a benchmarking course will vary accordingly. See the following section on "Supplemental Training and Activities to Support Benchmarking" for content ideas. A sample of a benchmarking course content is illustrated by the following outline:

I. OVERVIEW
   A. What is benchmarking?
   B. Why benchmark?
   C. When to benchmark?
II. STEPS IN THE BENCHMARKING MODEL
   A. Step 1
      (See Section 6, "Comparing Process Models for Benchmarking," for a description of alternative benchmarking process models.)
   B. Step N
III. APPLICATION OF BENCHMARKING
   A. Planning the next steps for your organization
   B. Course evaluation and follow up

For additional content ideas refer to Table 5-1, which outlines the content of several public benchmarking courses.

SUPPLEMENTAL TRAINING ACTIVITIES TO SUPPORT BENCHMARKING

Benchmarking is often referred to as an "advanced TQM tool." While benchmarking is considered to be advanced, the process is not overly complicated. Indeed, each step in the benchmarking process is straightforward and logical. The difficult aspect of benchmarking is focusing the energy, resources, and discipline to start and complete a study.

Effective benchmarking does require some basic information: knowledge of who your customers are, what your critical success factors (CSFs) are, and which of your processes impact your customer's CSFs. In addition, detailed process knowledge, flowcharts or diagrams, and metrics are essential to provide a basis of comparison—the very essence of what benchmarking is about. Sadly, many U.S. organizations lack these prerequisites, and this makes benchmarking an "advanced TQM tool."

When customer knowledge, CSFs, process knowledge, and metrics are not in place within an organization, then training and other efforts must be initiated to put them in place. This should occur before the initiation of large-scale benchmarking activities. This advice may be reminiscent of the famous recipe for Elephant Stew: Step 1 — get an elephant. It may delay the initiation of benchmarking in many organizations, but the delay is surely preferable to the inevitable failure of efforts to benchmark without customer or process knowledge.

One survey item sought to clarify the skills that are needed for successful benchmarking. The skills listed below can be used as an organizational self-examination tool to reveal which skills should be included in your benchmarking course. Some organizations reduce the time in their benchmarking course by ensuring that the needed skills are available separately. Figure 5-3 shows the survey results. Your company's training manager can direct you to sources of training in these skills areas.

Additional benchmarking-related skills have been identified by experienced benchmarkers: surveying (written, telephone, and mail), interview techniques (data gathering) and facility touring. These skills have been successfully addressed by several organizations by adding written appendixes to their benchmarking skills courses.

Negotiating	3.5
Writing	3.5
Conducting meetings	3.8
Research	3.8
Other	4.0
Problem solving	4.0
Interpersonal relations	4.2
Team building	4.2
Communications	4.5
Process analysis	4.6

Note: These figures are based on the survey average of a five-point rating scale, with five referring to the skills of most importance.

Figure 5-3. How Would You Rate the Importance of the Following Skills for Benchmarking Study Participants?

Another item identifies several products and tools that can be invaluable to a benchmarking function. Figure 5-4 lists these support products and tools. Notice that 56.8 percent of the respondents indicated that training is an essential enabler for benchmarking.

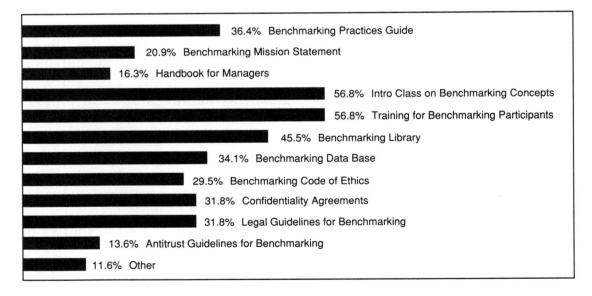

- 36.4% Benchmarking Practices Guide
- 20.9% Benchmarking Mission Statement
- 16.3% Handbook for Managers
- 56.8% Intro Class on Benchmarking Concepts
- 56.8% Training for Benchmarking Participants
- 45.5% Benchmarking Library
- 34.1% Benchmarking Data Base
- 29.5% Benchmarking Code of Ethics
- 31.8% Confidentiality Agreements
- 31.8% Legal Guidelines for Benchmarking
- 13.6% Antitrust Guidelines for Benchmarking
- 11.6% Other

Figure 5-4. Which of the Following Has Your Company Developed to Support Your Benchmarking Effort?

Additional topics for benchmark-related training and support can be found in Figure 5-5, which looks at data-gathering methods.

Consultants	2.1
Contracting with research organizations	2.1
Trade associations	2.8
Contracting with industry experts	3.0
Administering written surveys	3.4
Site visits	3.6
Conducting telephone interviews	3.7
Researching journals	3.8
Networking	4.0
Reading articles	4.1
Brainstorming with team members	4.7

Note: These figures are based on the survey average of a five-point rating scale, with five referring to the most frequently used methods.

Figure 5-5. For Each of the Following Data Gathering Methods, Indicate How Frequently They Are Used in Benchmarking Studies

SPECIAL CONSIDERATIONS

According to the survey, one almost universal requirement for benchmarking training is the use of teams. Responses indicate that 93.6 percent of responding organizations use teams to conduct benchmarking studies (see Figure 5-6).

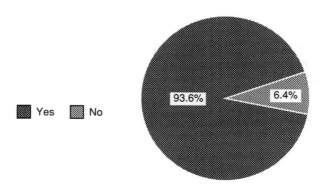

Figure 5-6. Do You Utilize a Team Approach?

This may explain why soft skills such as conducting meetings, interpersonal relations, team building, and communications were highly rated in the survey (see Figure 5-3).

The typical size of a benchmarking study team (Figure 5-7) is in the same range as employee involvement teams, problem-solving teams or quality circles: generally four to eight, and most often four to five, members.

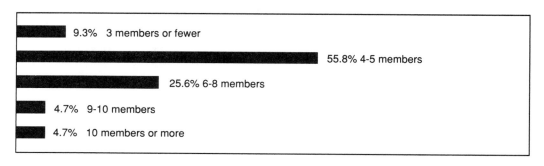

Figure 5-7. How Many Team Members Comprise a Typical Team?

These facts need to be taken into account when a benchmarking training program is designed. Since many of the topics covered in the training are skills, sufficient time and exercises to learn and practice should be provided. Most benchmarking skills programs report use of case studies and team exercises.

The near-universal use of teams to conduct benchmark studies suggests that a successful benchmarking management course should address the identification and maintenance of teams. Several corporations structure their benchmarking skills workshops so actual teams can attend together. Some companies supplement these teams with professional benchmarking facilitators whose roles are to maintain the correct protocol and process of benchmarking. This practice can effectively further team participation and allow real benchmarking study issues to be discussed and resolved. Starting a study project with a training experience is much more efficient than dealing with the issues after the study has commenced.

Course designs involving teams place an additional burden of expertise upon the instructor. He or she needs to use specific knowledge of the client organization to guide the teams toward success. The instructor must also have a solid base of organizational development skills to facilitate team building and conflict resolution in class. This may explain the 35.1 percent of survey respondents who indicate it takes over 40 hours of training to be ready to instruct benchmarking (see Figure 5-4).

ENSURING SUCCESS

A proven method of ensuring the success of any process or organizational initiative is to study the causes of failure and take steps not to repeat them yourself. In fact that is often the purpose of a benchmarking study. Figure 5-8 shows causes of benchmarking study failures.

Poor planning	3.78
No top management support	3.76
No process owner involved	3.56
Insufficient benchmarking skills	3.54
Low priority	3.14
Results not believed	2.93
Lack of interest	2.76
Lack of funding	2.68
Poor teamwork	2.67
Personnel turnover	2.20
No better practices found	2.17
Interpersonal conflicts	2.07

Note: Survey respondents were asked to rate the factors identified above on a five-point scale to indicate the significance of the factor's contribution to an unsuccessful benchmarking study. Multiple answers were not allowed.

Figure 5-8. In Your Company's Experience, When a Benchmarking Study and Implementation Are *Not* Successful, to What Extents Are the Following Factors the Cause?

The top four causes of failure stand out from the rest by a considerable margin: poor planning, no top-management support, no process-owner involved, and insufficient benchmarking skills. All four can be addressed, and their risks reduced, if the training products previously described are carefully crafted and skillfully executed. They should be fully integrated into the organization's ongoing continuous improvement strategies and fit within the organization's culture.

Section 6
Comparing Process Models
for Benchmarking

- Introduction
- Fundamental Definitions
- Benchmarking Objective
- Benchmarking Template
- A Meta-Model for Benchmarking
- Reengineering and Process Thinking
- Process Template
- Process Taxonomy
- Notes

INTRODUCTION

Two characteristics of a profession are a common vocabulary and a structured approach or methodology. These two elements allow broad communication and establish a common basis for dialogue with others in the same profession. Benchmarking is coming of age as a process and a profession; therefore, there is a current need for a common vocabulary and approach. This section presents terminology and benchmarking process methods applied by member companies of the Design Steering Committee of the International Benchmarking Clearinghouse. It presents a generic process model for benchmarking that can be used to compare individual company process benchmarking models with the more general elements. Finally, this section describes areas that require further professional development and investigation: process templates, process and metric taxonomies, and the use of benchmarking to support organizational reengineering.

FUNDAMENTAL DEFINITIONS

Four terms must be defined to provide a common perspective on benchmarking: process, model, benchmark, and benchmarking. Operational definitions of these terms are presented below.

Process: A logical series of interrelated transactions that convert inputs into results or outputs. Processes consume resources and require standards and documentation for repeatable performance. Processes respond to control systems that direct the quality, rate, and cost of performance. All processes can be measured by the efficiency and effectiveness of their external results and internal performance. Gilbert Pall defines a business process as a "logical organization of people, materials, energy, equipment, and procedures into work activities designed to produce a specified end result."[1]

Model: A description, representation, or analogy that is used to help visualize something that cannot be directly observed. A model forms a pattern

---

This section was strongly influenced by Bob Camp of Xerox. At the November 19, 1991, meeting of the Design Steering Committee, Bob outlined future benchmarking challenges. Those challenges included the need for a generic process model, common vocabulary, process templates, and a process taxonomy. That "process classification" has since been developed by the Clearinghouse and is available through APQC.

from which something can be understood and produced in full scale. A process model is typically a graphic representation of the process sequence, organizational structure, or data flows that together describe the functionality of the process.

Benchmark: A "best-in-class" achievement. This achievement is a measured reference point or recognized standard of excellence against which similar things are measured.

Benchmarking: The process of continuously comparing and measuring an organization with business leaders anywhere in the world to gain information that will help the organization take action to improve its performance. Benchmarking is a systematic and continuous process that requires identification of practices, methods, or actions that will enable performance improvement relative to the benchmark.

Process Benchmarking: The benchmarking of discrete process performance and functionality against organizations that lead in those processes. Process benchmarking seeks the best practice for conducting a particular business process after validating that the benchmarked performance of that process is, indeed, world class. Once the best practice is understood, then it may be adapted and improved for application to another organization.

BENCHMARKING OBJECTIVE

The objective of benchmarking is to provide a goal for realistic process improvement and an understanding of changes necessary to facilitate that improvement. Benchmarking entails a bias for action that can lead to breakthroughs and continuous improvements in products, processes, and services. The application of benchmarking-study findings should produce increased customer satisfaction and improved competitive advantage.

BENCHMARKING TEMPLATE

During the development of process for the International Benchmarking Clearinghouse, the American Productivity & Quality Center (APQC) conducted a survey of the 87 member companies of the Design Steering Committee. One question asked these companies to describe their model for the process of benchmarking. The results were unusual. The number of steps that were described ranged from 4 to 33. The distribution of steps is shown in Table 6-1.

Table 6-1. Distribution of Steps

Number of Steps	Number of Companies	Percent
4	6	14
5	3	7
6	7	17
7	8	19
8	4	10
9	3	7
10	8	19
12	2	5
33	1	2

*The total number of respondents to this question was 42.

It is difficult to communicate among companies where variety exists in the definition of their approach to benchmarking. Recognizing the need for improved communication, four companies that have been active in benchmarking collaborated to develop a general template for benchmarking. These companies — The Boeing Corporation, Digital Equipment Corporation, Motorola, Inc., and Xerox Corporation — created a four-quadrant model to explain what benchmarking is about. A template is a pattern that can be used as a guide for defining a business process. This template establishes a general context for developing a process model that indicates the specific sequence of actions required to complete the benchmarking process (see Figure 6-1).

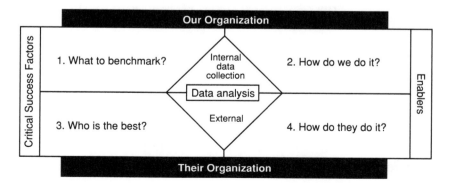

Figure 6-1. Benchmarking Process Template

This template also provides a perspective on the considerations that need to be made while benchmarking is conducted, and it introduces two additional terms that need to be defined: critical success factors and enablers.

Critical Success Factors (CSFs): Those characteristics, conditions, or variables that have a direct influence on your customer's satisfaction, and therefore your own success. If the process performance satisfies CSFs, then your company's competitive performance will be successful and your business will flourish.

Enablers: Those processes, practices, or methods that make possible the "best-in-class" performance. While performance benchmarks measure the successful execution of a process, enablers tell the reasons behind the successful implementation: the system, method, document, training, or techniques that facilitate the implementation of the process.

The template that these four companies developed has four quadrants, linked by the processes of data collection and analysis. What happens in each of these four quadrants? Perhaps the best way to explain is to pose the questions that a team would ask when it is in each of these quadrants.

First Quadrant: What to Benchmark?

- Have you identified the critical success factors for the business?
- Have you named a team leader and empowered the leader to form a team and benchmark?
- Have you selected the right thing to tackle: problem area to address, result to achieve, etc.?
- Will a change in this process be perceived by our customers as a benefit?

Second Quadrant: How Do We Do It?

- Have you mapped your process, and do you understand how you are doing it?
- Do you have operational definitions for all key terms?
- Will you be able to compare your measurements with others and make sense from the result?

Third Quadrant: Who Is the Best-in-Class?

- What companies perform this process better than you do?
- What global company, independent of industry, is the best at performing this process?
- What is your internal best-in-class process performance?

Fourth Quadrant: How Do They Do It?

- What is their process?
- What is their performance goal?
- How do they measure process performance?
- Can you verify their process results?
- What enables the performance of their process?

How can the APQC survey responses and this template be used to develop a process model of benchmarking that applies to a broad range of organizations? The Deming Cycle in quality is a generic four-step approach to management. It is named after its leading proponent, Dr. W. Edwards Deming. Most of the specific company models map into Deming's four steps: Plan, Do, Check, and Act. Five company models and their relationship to the four-step process model as developed by the APQC are shown in Table 6-2.

One observation from studying the various company approaches is that they fall into four general steps that may be labeled Plan, Collect, Analyze, and Improve — altering the labels of the Deming Cycle to apply more directly to the benchmarking process. The five most popular model types, representing 79 percent of the survey responses, are represented here.

Several models were used by a number of companies, and it was possible to identify source models for benchmarking — the Xerox ten-step and the Westinghouse seven-step model tied for the highest number of "votes" and were followed closely by the GOAL/QPC and APQC six-step model.

Table 6-2. Five Company Models

Four-Step Process Model	Plan	Collect	Analyze	Improve
1. Prepare to benchmark 2. Research processes 3. Document best practice 4. Report and implement	✔	✔	✔	✔

Six-Step Process Model	Plan	Collect	Analyze	Improve
1. Plan 2. Research 3. Observe 4. Analyze 5. Adapt 6. Improve	✔	✔ ✔	✔	✔ ✔

Seven-Step Process Model	Plan	Collect	Analyze	Improve

1. Determine functions or processes
   to benchmark
2. Identify key performance variables
3. Identify best-in-class companies
4. Measure performance
5. Compare performance and
   estimate gaps
6. Specify improvement
7. Implement and monitor results
	✔
	✔
	✔
		✔	✔	✔
				✔

Eight-Step Process Model	Plan	Collect	Analyze	Improve
1. Define business issue 2. Definte what to benchmark 3. Define benchmark measures 4. Determine who to benchmark 5. Acquire data 6. Compare performance 7. Identify actions to close the gap 8. Implement improvements and monitor results	✔ ✔ ✔ ✔	✔	✔ ✔	✔

Ten-Step Process Model	Plan	Collect	Analyze	Improve
1. Identify process 2. Identify partner 3. Collect data 4. Determine gap 5. Project future performance 6. Gain support 7. Set goals 8. Develop plans 9. Implement plans 10. Recalibrate benchmarks	✔ ✔	✔	✔ ✔	✔ ✔ ✔ ✔ ✔

A META-MODEL FOR BENCHMARKING

To clarify the sequence of activities that occur during the benchmarking process, each of these four steps in the generic benchmarking model is identified in terms of the actions or areas to address for the benchmarking team during that step:

Planning a Benchmarking Project

- Select the processes to benchmark.
- Gain participation of the process owner.
- Select the leader for the benchmarking team and identify the team for benchmarking.
- Identify the process customer's profile and set of expectations.
- Analyze process flow and process performance measures.
- Document and flow diagram the process.
- Identify generic versions of the process-performance measures.
- Select the critical success factors to benchmark.
- Establish the data-collection method.

Collecting Data

- Collect internal process data.
- Research similar processes through secondary sources.
- Identify best-in-class.
- Plan data collection.
- Develop survey or interview guide.
- Select the processes to benchmark.
- Gain participation of the process owner.
- Select the leader for the benchmarking team and identify the team for benchmarking.
- Identify the process customer profile and their set of expectations.
- Analyze process flow and process-performance measures.
- Contact benchmarking partners and gain participation.
- Collect preliminary data.
- Make on-site observations.

Analyzing Data for Performance Gaps and Enablers

- Organize and reformat the data to permit identification of performance gaps.
- Normalize performance to a common base.
- Compare current performance against the benchmark.
- Identify performance gaps and their causes, and highlight the reason that the gap exists.
- Project the performance three to five years into the future.
- Develop "best practice" case studies.
- Isolate process enablers that correlate to process improvements.
- Evaluate the nature of the process enablers and best practices to determine their adaptability to your culture.

Improving by Adapting Process Enablers and Best Practices

- Set goals to reduce, meet, and then exceed the performance gap.
- Modify process enablers and best practices to meet your company culture and organizational structure.
- Gain acceptance, support, commitment, and ownership for changes required.
- Develop an action plan.
- Commit the resources required for implementation.
- Implement the plan.
- Monitor and report progress toward the goal.
- Identify opportunities for future benchmarking and recalibrate the measure regularly.

This four-step process benchmarking model is compatible with change processes used in total quality management (TQM). The two basic strategic change processes are continuous improvement (called *kaizen* in Japanese) and breakthrough improvement (called *hoshin kanri* in Japanese and translated as policy deployment). In addition to these two methods, reengineering has come to be recognized as a third change mechanism that is more radical than either of the TQM change processes. How is reengineering related to benchmarking change activities?

REENGINEERING AND PROCESS THINKING

Over the years many business processes have been changed by "tweaking the system" — a kind of creeping change where major shifts in process activity have not occurred. In change mechanisms of this sort there is a danger of failing to eliminate all of the remnants of the old process that are no longer required. This is also a potential problem with implementing action plans for breakthrough improvements required to meet new benchmarking goals.

Process thinking is a style of thinking that evaluates actions and activities in relation to their processes. Process thinking is also fundamental to reengineering. Reengineering starts with business process redesign as the first step. Business process redesign is the analysis and design of work flows and processes within and between organizations. Business process redesign is cross-functional and has implications across the organization.

Reengineering involves the radical redesign of business processes, organizational structures, management systems, and values of an organization to achieve breakthroughs in business performance. At the core of reengineering is the concept of discontinuous thinking — recognizing and breaking away from the outdated rules and fundamental assumptions that are the foundation of daily operations. Reengineering is effective when the process is fundamentally flawed. However, redesigning the process and capitalizing on information technology improvements are often not enough. Michael Hammer proposed a set of rules of reengineering:[2]

- Organize around outcomes, not tasks.
- Have those who use the output of the process perform the process.
- Subsume information-processing work into the real work that produces the information.
- Treat geographically dispersed resources as though they were centralized.
- Link parallel activities instead of integrating their results.
- Put the decision point where the work is performed, and build control into the process.
- Capture information once and at the source.

The relationship of reengineering with process benchmarking will continue to develop as both of these processes mature. Fundamental to both are two related tools: a process template and process taxonomies.

PROCESS TEMPLATE

A process template is a pattern that can be used as a guide for defining a business process. It defines the process using functional, organizational, and conceptual descriptions. Process templates are used to communicate the essential information about a process, and they are used in the Clearinghouse database of process examples. Data elements in a process template include process definitions, process metrics, and actual process performance measures. A prototype process template is illustrated in Table 6-3.

Table 6-3. General Process Template

Company name (optional) ——————————— Company contact (optional) ———————
Site location (optional)————————————— Phone number (optional)————————————

Template Element	Definition
Process Name	Generic Process Name

Process definition
  Process description
  Organization chart
  Process flowchart
	Information required to understand the conceptual, organizational, and functional relationships of the target process

Process performance measures
  Quality
  Cost
  Cycle time
	Metrics and nominalized performance
	
	Internal performance improvement trends

Process outputs and customers	External performance measures
Process inputs and suppliers	Incoming performance measures

Process resources
  Standards and procedures
  Personnel training
  Capital expense budget
  Equipment and information systems
  Physical configuration
	Information required to understand the resources invested in the process and the process support requirements for obtaining the specified performance.

Process enablers and attributes	Implementation features and common characteristics of world-class processes.

PROCESS TAXONOMY

A process taxonomy is a systematic and orderly classification of business processes according to their natural relationships. The fundamental structure for understanding relationships among business processes is systems thinking, or the ability to look at the whole, rather than the parts, of a set of processes. The act of developing a process taxonomy is sometimes called business system decomposition. One way of approaching this subject is to look at businesses according to their five nested levels of performance: system, process, activity, step, and task. A system is a set of processes; processes are composed of activities; activities are a sequence of steps; and each step is a set of tasks. An example of this hierarchical structure is shown in Figure 6-2 using a tree diagram.

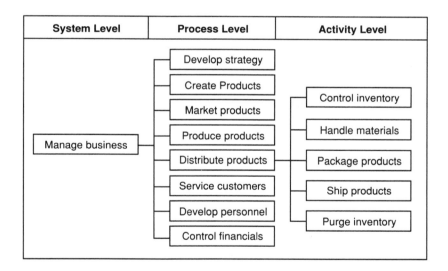

Figure 6-2. Creating a Generic Business Structure

A process taxonomy describes the relationship among the various functions and processes of an organization. At the activity level of this taxonomy, industry-specific process elements may be described in a format similar to the General Process Template. A matrix of process elements and industry types can be used to help translate industrial synonyms for process measures and names. This matrix would help benchmarkers since most benchmarking activity is focused on narrowly defined processes that occur at the activity level of the process taxonomy. Further development of process taxonomies, process templates, and reengineering applications for benchmarking are needed to make these tools and processes practical for benchmarkers.

NOTES

1. Business process management is addressed in Gilbert A. Pall, *Quality Process Management*, Englewood Cliffs, NJ: Prentice-Hall, 1987; and H. James Harrington, *Business Process Improvement: The Breakthrough Strategy for Total Quality, Productivity, and Competitiveness*, New York: McGraw-Hill, 1991.
2. Work redesign and process reengineering are introduced in Michael Hammer, "Reengineering Work: Don't Automate, Obliterate," *Harvard Business Review*, July-August 1990; Thomas H. Davenport and James E. Short, "The New Industrial Engineering: Information Technology and Business Process Redesign," *Sloan Management Review*, Summer 1990; and Gary K. Gulden and Robert H. Reck, "Combining Quality and Reengineering for Operational Superiority," *Indicators: Perspectives on Management of Information Technology*, September-October 1991.

Section 7
Finding Benchmark Information Through Secondary Research

- Introduction
- Basic Approach for Collecting Information
- Methods of Secondary Research
- Sources of Information
- Building a Basic Research Capability
- Data Bases for Business Information
- Twelve Basic Information Sources for Your Company's Library
- Developing a Continuous Information Monitoring System
- Additional Sources of Information

"There is very little that confidential sources can tell that is not accessible to an alert analyst who knows what he is looking for and knows how to find and use these sources."
Captain Ellis Zacharias
Secret Mission: The Story of an Intelligence Officer

INTRODUCTION

Secondary research is the practice of searching for information about a particular subject area from indirect sources. Although an important aspect of competitive market research, secondary research is also used in the second phase of a process benchmarking study. It is also the most confusing phase of the benchmarking process to individuals conducting their first benchmarking study. Why should a company conduct competitive research using secondary sources?

One good reason for conducting secondary research as a regular part of the business planning process is to avoid the ostrich syndrome. A business cannot afford to be ignorant of what is happening in its environment. Some companies call this practice environmental scanning. The underlying reason that a company conducts secondary research is to gain competitive advantage. The world is full of data in many forms, but until it is turned into useful, actionable information, it is of little value to a company. When data is converted into useful information, it becomes vital for many business applications: strategic planning, market research analysis and customer preference analysis for new product or service development, technology development scanning, and business and capital budget planning for development, investment, or acquisitions. For all of these applications, the data must be synthesized into relevant, timely, and accurate information to help direct the plans of a business. Types of data that need to be transformed include technical, product, market, customer, environmental, and competitive information. Companies should identify essential elements of information to determine the requirements for secondary research.

There are four phases of maturity in the evolution of business planning and its requirement for information:

1. Financial planning
2. Integration of sales forecasting with materials planning
3. Market research and analysis (industry analysis and product positioning)
4. Strategic and competitive management of change

The final phase of maturity in planning brings the strongest demand for integrated information management. In this phase of maturity, a company would integrate all competitive and business environmental information: market research, industry analysis, product positioning, customer satisfaction surveys, competitive product analysis, reverse engineering, and process benchmarking. An integrated information system provides a means for preventing surprises, either business threats or developmental opportunities, that could arise from current or potential business competitors.

The principal value of secondary research is to provide historical perspective and set a standard of comparison for a specific point in time. Secondary research has a built-in time delay that can be years old — even for current publications. For instance, the Union of Japanese Scientists and Engineers (JUSE) will release publications for English translation that were published in Japanese two to five years prior. Since secondary research does not provide the most current information about the activities of an organization, when time is of the essence and accurate information is required, a company should conduct reverse engineering, process benchmarking, or competitive intelligence. Following the process for secondary research does provide substantial background knowledge for process benchmarking and is therefore an important step in conducting a benchmarking study.

BASIC APPROACH FOR COLLECTING INFORMATION

What does it take to collect, analyze, and synthesize these types of data? It takes people who understand business processes, who possess insights into the sources of available data, who have the flexibility to seek creative ways to obtain information, to efficiently develop a plan or strategy for obtaining data, and to persist in their pursuit of the required data to produce the desired information.

The process for secondary research contains six steps:

1. *Requirements sorting:* The researcher determines the key words for searching data bases and library files.
2. *Data collection:* The researcher collects data from a variety of secondary sources based on the search requirements.
3. *Data sorting:* The data is compiled according to common themes and categories of information that present themselves from the data.
4. *Information analysis:* The researcher makes "sense" out of the data that has been collected.

5. *Business synthesis:* The researcher integrates the information gleaned from the data into the specific business situation of his or her company.
6. *Results presentation:* The results are communicated to the appropriate level of management for consideration and action.

Not many companies have reached full maturity in their use of secondary research methods. Companies may be sorted into four categories based on their ability to conduct secondary research:

- Company has no internal secondary research capability.
- Company has an internal library/research function that only provides information based upon specific user requests.
- Company strategically collects and applies information to support specific, requested management objectives.
- Company has developed an integrated, rationalized companywide data base, which is used to continuously monitor essential information elements.

METHODS OF SECONDARY RESEARCH

Many people first hear about secondary research in grade school when they learn how to use a library. Most of the principles are the same. The six-step process of secondary research presents several challenges for collecting information. It is necessary to become an information detective to discover the specific information needed to answer your business question. The basic question in most of these skills is: "What information do I need?" Some of the critical methods or skills that help to determine the answer include the following.

Developing Questionnaires and Key-Word Searches

Even when you are not conducting interviews for a specific search, it is often helpful to organize your thoughts about the search by developing a questionnaire. It provides a point of common reference for all interviews or investigations and helps to set the design of the key-word searches on electronic data bases. A questionnaire can be used as a basis for a phone survey, as a mailed survey form, or for directing the flow of a face-to-face meeting. The questions can provide a logical flow for the discussion, help to open the communication dialog, and ensure that specific information is requested.

The questionnaire also helps to organize the final report of the project. Key words are used to establish a selective dissemination of information that allows a researcher to place company names or subject matter topics into a data base and receive regular reports whenever the data base is updated. Most data bases have a "thesaurus" describing the topical labels and their synonyms that are available for key-word searches. The thesaurus will also typically include search tips to help you use the data base more competently. Most data base suppliers will sell their thesaurus in hard copy to potential subscribers for a nominal fee. Another tip is to take a training session in how to use the data base service. This training will provide you with the search methodology to make the data base more productive.

Finding a Business Library

A library is an essential resource for business information. If you do not have a business library within your own company, then you will need to obtain access to an external one. Business libraries exist throughout the country and may be found in graduate schools of business, public business libraries, corporate business libraries that are willing to conduct interbusiness searches, and the special libraries of research centers (such as the American Productivity & Quality Center's library, which specializes in quality and productivity). Consider your local resources. Universities with prestigious business schools will be able to meet most of your research needs. If you cannot locate an adequate business library, then look at the *Directory of Special Libraries and Information Centers,* described in a later subsection.

Knowing What Reference Materials Exist

Just as it is important to know your library, it is also important to know the major reference materials for your areas of interest. There are many directories and information services available for a researcher. The lists of sources in later subsections will provide good starting points for investigating and applying them to your specific industry. Knowledge of what is available is essential to beginning your research.

Using a Data Base

A data base is of no use unless you can get to what is inside it. Some of the considerations for using electronic data bases include how much of the data is in the data base (abstract or full text); what sources are used for the data base; what area the data base specializes in; how often and when the data base is updated; and what services it has available to support you in your searches. As the customer of the data base service, you may have access not only to special training, but also to expert assistance in setting up your "standard information requests" for regular reports. The data base service may provide consulting to help you build the most appropriate inquiry for searches.

Obtaining Government Documents

Government agencies publish thousands of documents each year that provide information about businesses. These documents are accessible directly from the government agencies or may be obtained from private retrieval firms that will conduct a custom search for specific materials when you are not sure of your requirements. One of these agencies, the Washington Service Bureau, provides a broad degree of services for retrieval of information from all government agencies.

SOURCES OF INFORMATION

A professional conducting secondary research must know not only the sources of information, but must also be able to answer: "What kind of information is available?"

To answer this question, a researcher needs to have a good command of the potential sources of information about businesses. A basic set of information sources is listed below along with the types of information that you can expect to find.

- *Business press:* This is an excellent source of current announcements: management changes, new product introductions, major litigation, business strategy, and analysis articles on the business and how it compares to major competitors.

- *Trade press/technical journals:* These sources provide comparative technical information about the relative merits of the industry's products and services. Technical journals can provide detailed articles by engineers about specific elements of design on leading technologies that are being used in current products. These sources can also provide detailed analyses of the capabilities of new products and services. In addition, they will contain information from customer surveys and opinion polls.
- *Government reports:* The Department of Commerce publishes detailed information on industry performance status and trends relative to American and foreign businesses.
- *Public financial statements:* These filings provide the detail behind the annual report and can be used for analyzing internal business efficiency.
- *Association materials/conference proceedings and journals:* Industry associations conduct conferences and publish materials that reflect the current technical, environmental, and business issues of that industry.
- *Data bases, clipping services, and information networks:* These tools provide consolidated information from many sources and may be customized to meet your specific business needs.

BUILDING A BASIC RESEARCH CAPABILITY

It takes three to five years to build a research capability that meets all of a company's external information needs. In some smaller companies, the expense of this investment may not be warranted, and alternative information retrieval services and reference library capabilities need to be found. If a research library is warranted, you may want to start by building a basic research capability and expanding as your need grows. A good first step would be to monitor the financial, technical, and business news about your principal competitors. The next steps could be to:

- Develop a reporting structure and system of business measures for using competitive information in the company's strategic plan.
- Build a capability to respond to specific information search requests.
- Create the organization and reference materials to continue this service on a long-term basis.

If you decide to make secondary research and competitive intelligence part of your company's information management activities, then you will want to build a basic library to help initiate your information search.

DATA BASES FOR BUSINESS INFORMATION

Your library should also have access to some of the basic data bases of business information. Additional data bases will be available through DIALOG and CompuServe, which are fundamental information network tools for business research. Some specialty capabilities include:

- *DRI/McGraw-Hill:* DRI provides on-line information on global economic and financial conditions and trends.
- *NEWSNET:* This on-line service provides full-text articles from over 420 news services and includes special services such as Bechtel SEC Filings Index, TRW Business Profiles, and NewsFlash electronic clipping services.
- *NEXIS:* This Mead Data Central product provides financial information on company filings (10K, etc.) and articles from more than 650 news, business, government, financial, trade, and technical sources.
- *World Patents Index/World Patents Index (Latest):* This on-line service from Derwent Publications provides listings of over 2.5 million patent documents from 24 countries. This data base should be searched by an individual who understands its structure and who is experienced in conducting a Derwent patent search.

TWELVE BASIC INFORMATION SOURCES FOR YOUR COMPANY'S LIBRARY

Some companies may want to move from the first level of maturity in their ability to conduct secondary research. This decision is not inexpensive. The following source materials for a "secondary research starter kit" cost almost $10,000 to purchase. You may decide that you want to find a business library that contains these works instead of developing your own library. Nevertheless, should you make the decision to move ahead, these reference books make a great start on an internal reference library. (Source addresses are listed at the end of this section.)

1. *Standard & Poor's Register of Corporations, Directors and Executives:* This annual three-volume listing of basic information about corporations and business executives is a research *must* for locating companies. Supplemental information is provided in April, July, and September.
2. *Thomas Register of American Manufacturers:* This annual 26-volume set is the standard guide for buying and selling products in America (available on DIALOG).
3. *Principal International Businesses:* This annual listing of the principal public and private companies in 133 countries is published by Dun & Bradstreet (available on DIALOG).
4. *Directories in Print:* This annual Gale Research Company directory lists over 10,000 business and industrial directories. Almost every industry has a directory that provides a detailed overview of the industry and business-specific performance statistics.
5. *Encyclopedia of Associations:* This annual Gale Research book lists publications of business, trade, and professional associations. Updated information is provided in December.
6. *Subject Directory of Special Libraries and Information Centers:* This annual Gale Research book provides information about company libraries and the libraries at research centers, associations, and unions.
7. *Directory of On-line Data Bases:* Gale has compiled a descriptive semi-annual listing of on-line data bases and services for locating specific types of information.
8. *Moody's Manuals:* Moody's Investors Service annually publishes eight financial manuals that provide public financial information about specific organizations in the United States as well as internationally. The most widely used manual is *Moody's Industrial Manual*, containing corporate history, capital structure, financial statements, and a discussion and analysis of management. Manuals are updated twice a week. Moody's has its own electronic information service, and their weekly news bulletins are available on DIALOG. News reports are also updated twice a week.
9. *Value Line Investment Surveys:* Value Line is a weekly investment advisory service that provides an annual financial analysis of 1,700 stocks from 95 industries (available on VALUE LINE DATA BASE II and CompuServe).

10. *Business Periodicals Index:* This monthly index (except in August), published by H.W. Wilson Company, abstracts information that appears about companies in the most important business journals (available on DIALOG). A bound annual is sent out at the end of the year.

11. *Wall Street Transcript:* This service provides information about specific companies and industries from articles and columns published by Dow Jones in the *Wall Street Journal* (available on-line from Dow Jones News/Retrieval and in microfilm from University Microfilms International). Transcripts from the four most recent shows are always available, with less than a one week lag time.

12. *U.S. Industrial Outlook:* This annual Department of Commerce publication tracks the trends in American business. The Washington Service Bureau retrieves government publications.

In addition to these reference books on secondary research, you will want to have a good collection of instructional materials on secondary research methods and competitive intelligence. A list at the end of this publication provides an introduction to this topic.

DEVELOPING A CONTINUOUS INFORMATION MONITORING SYSTEM

Benchmarking is a process that supports continuous business improvement. Supporting continuous improvement implies that information sources need a continuous stream of business data for analysis. One mark of the mature use of secondary research is the development of an integrated, rationalized, companywide data base. This analytical process scans electronic data bases for news items, financial reports, technical developments, and governmental activities. It uses a company-specific, key-word data model that fits an established criterion for critical data related to key business processes. The result of this scanning is the regular distribution of the external data to the company's business planners. These essential elements of information are then consolidated and reported to management. When this information stream indicates significant changes in the business situation, a process benchmarking study is triggered to understand the nature of the change. Naturally, the key-word data model includes companies that are benchmarking targets and not just competitors.

The acquisition and analysis of data; conversion of data into economically, operationally, and pragmatically viable information; and the presentation of current business situations and actionable alternatives to management form the core values of a business's continuous information-monitoring system.

ADDITIONAL SOURCES OF INFORMATION

For further information about secondary research and competitive intelligence:

1. Leonard M. Fuld, *Competitor Intelligence: How to Get It - How to Use It*, New York: John Wiley & Sons, 1985.
2. Leonard M. Fuld, *Monitoring the Competition: Finding Out What's Really Going On Over There*, New York: John Wiley & Sons, 1987.
3. William L. Sammon, Mark A. Kurland, and Robert Spitalnic, *Business Competitor Intelligence: Methods for Collecting, Organizing, and Using Information*, New York: John Wiley & Sons, 1984.
4. Kirk W.M. Tyson, *Business Intelligence: Putting It All Together*, Lombard, IL: Leading Edge Publications, 1986.
5. Washington Researchers, Ltd., *How to Find Information About Companies*, Washington, DC: Researchers Publishing, 1991.

For information on ordering the publications in the "secondary research starter kit":

1. CompuServe Information Service
   5000 Arlington Center Boulevard
   Columbus, OH 43220
   (800) 848-8199

2. DIALOG Information Services, Inc.
   3460 Hillview Avenue
   Palo Alto, CA 94304
   (800) 334-2564

3. Dow Jones & Company, Inc.
   P.O. Box 300
   Princeton, NJ 08543
   (609) 452-1511

4. Dun & Bradstreet
   Three Sylvan Way
   Parsippany, NJ 07054
   (800) 526-0651

5. Gale Research Company
   835 Penobscot Building
   Detroit, MI 48226
   (800) 877-4253

6. H.W. Wilson Company
   950 University Avenue
   Bronx, NY 10452
   (212) 588-8400

7. Moody's Investors Service, Inc.
   99 Church Street
   New York, NY 10007
   (800) 342-5647

8. Standard & Poor's Corporation
   25 Broadway
   New York, NY 10004
   (212) 208-8000

9. Thomas Publishing Company
   One Pennsylvania Plaza
   New York, NY 10119
   (212) 695-0500

10. University Microfilms, International
    300 North Zeeb Road
    Ann Arbor, MI 48106
    (800) 521-0600

11. U.S. Department of Commerce
    Industry and Trade Administration
    Washington, DC 20230
    (202) 277-3608

12. Value Line Inc.
    711 Third Avenue
    New York, NY 10017
    (212) 687-3965

13. Washington Service Bureau
    1225 Connecticut Avenue, NW
    Washington, DC 20036
    (202) 833-9200

    For additional information about referenced data base services:

1. Derwent Publications
   Rochdale House
   128 Theobalds Road
   London WC1X 8RP
   England

2. DRI/McGraw-Hill
   24 Hartwell Avenue
   Lexington, MA 02173
   (617) 863-5100

3. Mead Data Central
   P.O. Box 933
   Dayton, OH 45401
   (800) 227-4908

4. NEWSNET
   945 Haverford Road
   Bryn Mawr, PA 19010
   (800) 345-1301

Section 8
Assessing Quality Maturity: Applying Baldrige, Deming, and ISO 9000 Criteria for Internal Assessment

- Executive Summary
- Assessing Quality Maturity
- The Baldrige Award Process
- Comparison of 1991 Quality and Productivity Award Criteria
- Analysis of Alternative Approaches to Internal Assessment
- ISO 9000 Requirements
- Conclusion
- Notes

"I would lay it down as a basic principle of human organization that the individuals who hold the reins of power in any enterprise cannot trust themselves to be adequately self-critical. For those in power the danger of self-deception is very great, the danger of failing to see the problems or refusing to see them is ever-present. And the only protection is to create an atmosphere in which anyone can speak up."
John W. Gardner
"How to Prevent Organizational Dry Rot"
Harper's Magazine, October 1965

EXECUTIVE SUMMARY

Study Approach

This study by the staff of the American Productivity & Quality Center (APQC) evaluates alternative approaches for internal assessment systems. The APQC benchmarked approaches to the internal assessment of quality management systems in four phases. The first phase analyzes the 1991 Malcolm Baldrige National Quality Award criteria. The second phase compares the 1991 award criteria with the following quality awards: the Deming Prize, the Malcolm Baldrige National Quality Award, the President's Award for Quality and Productivity Improvement, the George M. Low Trophy (NASA's Productivity and Excellence Award), and the Shigeo Shingo Prize for Excellence in American Manufacturing. The third phase compares the internal implementation approaches of 23 companies selected from American industry for their recognized formal assessment systems. The fourth phase evaluates the integration of the requirements of ISO 9004 with the Baldrige criteria. An additional section examines the 1992 Baldrige criteria.

Major Study Findings

1. The five quality awards considered in this paper differed significantly in their award criteria and scoring guidelines. Although the 1991 Baldrige Award criteria were considered the most complete of the five awards, there is still room for improvement.
2. The weighting of the categories among the various awards indicates their focus for applicant recognition: the Shingo Prize focuses on process control at the shop-floor level with half of its points assigned to this area,

while the Baldrige Award, President's Award, and NASA Award recognize a broader area of quality performance. The Deming Application Prize uses a prescriptive criteria system but applies the same criteria to all areas of the company to achieve breadth of application.

3. Of the 23 companies studied, 5 used self-assessment surveys, 1 combined a self-assessment survey with an internal Baldrige-like assessment, 9 used the Baldrige assessment materials without change, and 8 customized the Baldrige process or criteria for their own internal application.

4. The biggest area for improvement in internal company assessment systems is the calibration of individual examiner scoring. One company reported spreads greater than 400 points among examiners. This is consistent with the scores submitted by individuals selected for the Malcolm Baldrige National Quality Award Board of Examiners, but not yet trained. A key intent of the examiner training is to calibrate the examiners to recognize when performance is above or below the 50 percent level of the scoring guidelines.

5. While the ISO 9004 Quality System Guidelines and the Malcolm Baldrige National Quality Award criteria have many examination items in common, the Baldrige criteria are more complete in general. In the process control area, however, ISO 9004 tends to be more prescriptive than the Baldrige Award.

6. For the 1992 Baldrige Award, administrators have strengthened the explanation of several examination items. Specifically, the criteria for Category Six have been broadened to provide an increased focus on business operating results.

7. Each company must evaluate its own quality system requirement in light of its customers' needs. This paper provides a basis for that assessment and indicates that the Baldrige criteria are the most comprehensive set of criteria for internal quality assessments.

Study Objective

In 1987, President Ronald Reagan signed the Malcolm Baldrige National Quality Improvement Act, which established a national award to recognize quality improvement among manufacturing, service, and small businesses. The act did not describe the scoring system, judging process, or criteria for evaluating applications. The examination criteria were developed by a group of recognized quality professionals who volunteered their services to establish this operational statement of quality. The examination criteria have become an operational definition of total quality management (TQM) and the wide distribution of the application guidelines has exposed many senior managers to the Baldrige definition of TQM.

The Malcolm Baldrige National Quality Award was not the first prestigious quality award. That distinction goes to the Deming Application Prize of the Union of Japanese Scientists and Engineers (JUSE). Initiated in 1951 and named after W. Edwards Deming, the American quality guru who helped to begin the Japanese quality movement, the Deming Prize has long been recognized as an indicator of excellence in business. In a 1983 study by Dr. Noriaki Kano of Deming recipients' business performance, it was observed that the Deming Prize winners enjoyed a 3 to 6 percent range of advantage in annual return on net assets over nonwinners from the same industry during the decade of the 1970s.[1]

While the Deming Prize is focused on statistical process control as the fundamental building block of quality (see the summary of award criteria in Appendix B), the Baldrige Award recognizes customer satisfaction as the foundation of quality and applies quality methods to business management. Other quality and productivity awards with slightly different intent and criteria have been introduced to recognize improvement in particular areas:

- The President's Award for Quality and Productivity Improvement
- The George M. Low Trophy, NASA's Productivity and Excellence Award
- The Shigeo Shingo Prize for Manufacturing Excellence

These awards have stimulated interest in a United States business community that thrives on competitive recognition. David A. Garvin, a professor of business administration at the Harvard Business School and a member of the Board of Overseers for the Malcolm Baldrige National Quality Award from 1988 to 1990, has described the Baldrige Award as "the most important catalyst for transforming American business."[2] The award gives managers a framework to assess their progress for achieving quality results that produce competitive performance. Indeed, the General Accounting Office (GAO) has published a report that evaluates the business competitiveness of 20 companies that were high scorers on the 1988 or 1989 Baldrige Award applications. While the results of the GAO study were limited by the sample size, the GAO did conclude that there is a cause-and-effect relationship between the TQM practices embodied in the Baldrige Award criteria and a business's market share, productivity, and customer satisfaction.[3]

ASSESSING QUALITY MATURITY

Purpose

This study was conducted by the APQC's International Benchmarking Clearinghouse staff in conjunction with the APQC Consulting Group. It analyzes the interrelationships between the evaluation items of the Baldrige Award criteria; assesses the similarities and differences of the various quality award criteria; and compares approaches of different companies for incorporating self-assessment methods into their company's quality improvement approach.

Study Methodology

This study was conducted by evaluating open literature and presentations made by companies at quality forums where they presented the details of their quality assessment approach. This study uses information that was presented from 1989 through mid-1992 and may not reflect the most current approach of any particular company. However, the company information is considered to be representative of self-assessment methods that use the Baldrige Award criteria approach. The study findings include both a matrix comparing company approaches and a summary of best practices that contains a detailed description of a model approach for integrating the Baldrige Award criteria into a companywide assessment program.

Organizations Evaluated

The International Benchmarking Clearinghouse is a service operated by APQC to improve business competitiveness through a network of organizations dedicated to sharing improvement opportunities through benchmarking. During the design phase of the Clearinghouse, a survey of 87 companies involved in establishing this benchmarking network was conducted. It was found that 74 percent of these companies were using the Malcolm Baldrige National Quality

Award criteria for self-assessment, even though only 51 percent planned on applying for the award within the next five years. Of these companies, 88 percent also ranked their competitive position as leaders in most of their markets.[4] Companies using benchmarking and applying the Baldrige Award criteria clearly perceive themselves as leaders in their respective markets.

APQC's benchmarking study includes Clearinghouse members as well as external companies. Information about the organizations listed in Figure 8-1 was either volunteered or obtained from an open literature search of public domain publications and is included in the analysis of internal assessment practices; however, specific company practices are not identified in the comparison matrix.

Baxter Healthcare	Hewlett-Packard	Procter & Gamble
Control Data	Houston Business Round Table	Sematech
Corning	Hughes	Texaco
DuPont	IBM	TVA
Eaton	Intel	Westinghouse
Ernst & Young	Kodak	Whirlpool
Florida Power & Light	Loral	Xerox
FMC	Phillips Petroleum	

Figure 8-1. Organizations Studied

Description of Assessment

Levels and Types of Assessment

One of the basic concepts of TQM is that of process ownership. Process ownership means accepting responsibility for the performance of your assigned processes. This responsibility includes assessing those processes to improve customer satisfaction and process capability. For an entire business, this responsibility for assessment rests with the senior management team.

Assessment versus Audit

What is the distinction between an assessment and an audit? An *audit* is formal evaluation of performance to a predetermined standard. The audit process results in organizational change toward improved performance. On other hand, an *assessment* is a comparison of your organization's performan some standard to determine where you stand, what strengths you can build upon, and what weaknesses or areas of improvement need to be addressed. The basic distinction between quality audits and quality assessments is two-fold: the degree of formality and the scope of the application.[5] The American Society for Quality Control (ASQC) has defined a *quality audit* as "a systematic examination of the acts and decisions of people with respect to quality, in order to independently verify or evaluate and report compliance to the operational requirements of the quality program or the specification or contract requirements of the product or service." ASQC has defined a *quality system audit* as "an independent assessment of the effectiveness of an organization's quality system.[6,7] Although they are called audits, the quality award evaluations are assessments of quality systems, not detailed audits of product or process quality assurance.

Criteria versus Standards

Another basic distinction between quality assessments and quality audits is the basis of comparison. An audit compares performance against standards that indicate a minimal level of acceptable performance. An assessment compares performance against criteria that are goal-oriented performance measurements. Criteria are used to encourage specifically desired behavior toward a stretch objective that drives an organization to higher levels of quality performance. All of the quality awards use criteria rather than standards as the basis of quality performance evaluation.

Japanese Internal Quality Auditing System

As part of their total quality efforts, Japanese companies embarked on what is called a presidential audit. This audit is intended to correct the obvious problem that senior managers often do not know the true state of their business. These audits are considered quality diagnoses (assessment) rather than quality control (QC) audits. The quality diagnosis is similar to a quality system audit as defined by the ASQC. The QC audit is a product, process, or material type of audit at the detailed level. The differences between these two types of assessment are significant.

A quality audit evaluates the process of quality control implementation against a recognized standard and documented quality assurance procedures. This audit focuses on the methods and procedures by which the quality of a given product or service is assured. It also checks to determine if the requirements of customers are satisfied. On a regular basis a quality audit will sample products as delivered to the marketplace to determine the effectiveness of the on-line, or internal, quality control methods. If a defect is detected in the quality assurance process during the quality audit, then corrective action is taken to eliminate the problem and prevent its recurrence. This type of auditing scheme is aimed at applying the Deming cycle of Plan, Do, Check, Act to the continuous management of quality in all aspects of the product or service delivery system. In a sense, the quality audit is a further development of quality inspection systems. Neither quality audits nor inspections will ensure long-term stability in a quality control system because they focus only on performance at a single point in time or for a specific event.

On the other hand, the quality diagnosis examines the management aspects of the implementation of the quality system. The quality diagnosis is an audit of the quality delivery process rather than the product or service delivery process. It evaluates the capability of an organization to take preventative measures against the recurrence of mistakes. In a sense it is a meta-quality audit, since it looks at the process of the quality audit. The quality audit is a business fundamental; however, the quality diagnosis is required to ensure long-term success in product or service delivery by auditing the quality system and the manner in which the quality system is operated.

Japanese companies use four approaches to internal quality diagnostic audits. These audits, internal self-assessments of the total quality system that are sometimes called TQC audits, include:

- *Presidential audit:* This is a TQC diagnosis conducted by the president of the company and the senior management team. The senior managers go to the operations and administrative areas to observe the results of quality assurance activities personally and to judge the effectiveness of the quality system.
- *Business unit audit:* This TQC diagnosis is conducted by the head of a business unit in a manner similar to a presidential audit.
- *Quality control audit:* The QC audit is conducted by the senior quality officer of the company and a team comprised of quality professionals. This audit helps to establish consistency in the quality methods and procedures used across the company.
- *Departmental quality audit:* The departmental quality audit is conducted by exchanging audit professionals among the various departments to

conduct self-assessments. This exchange ensures objectivity in the observations by preserving the independence of the auditor. This level of audit follows the same process as the presidential audit.

Presidential Audits

A presidential audit provides top management with direct evidence of the performance of the companywide quality control system. Komatsu, Ltd., was featured in a 1987 *Quality Progress* article for its method of conducting presidential audits.[9] At that time, Komatsu had practiced the presidential audit since 1976. Ryoichi Kawai, Komatsu's chairman of the board, personally conducts these annual reviews of each functional unit. This audit has three purposes:

- To determine whether the daily operations of each department is being managed according to the basic policy
- To determine how well the president's policies are being implemented
- To increase the communications between the auditors and the audited parties

Komatsu was guided in developing its presidential audit by Kaoru Ishikawa.[10] The parties being audited prepare a *jissetsu*, a summary report of the progress of the audited process, for each audit. This report is limited to two pages for each scheduled hour of the audit. It addresses the achievement of the quality performance targets for each stage of product development. Ishikawa taught Komatsu management that these audits should not only review the presented material, but should also request additional reference material to provide the detail that is missing in the *jissetsu*. The minutes of each audit meeting serve as the basis for the follow-up audit.

Another practice used in the presidential audit is to check the process as well as the results. In this way a company's implementation of total quality is evaluated as well as the results it achieves. Ishikawa and Kano both helped to prototype this type of TQC diagnosis in many of the more advanced companies, including Florida Power & Light, Ford, Hewlett-Packard, and Procter & Gamble. This TQC diagnosis served as a model for the Malcolm Baldrige National Quality Award.

Hierarchy of Japanese Quality Recognition

Japanese quality professionals have established a system that provides five levels of recognition for companies. The first level is reflected in the Japanese Industrial Standards (JIS) mark, which is a certification for quality control. The second is the Ministry of International Trade and Industry Award, which is offered at both the regional and national levels. The third level is the Deming Application Prize. The fourth level is the Japan Quality Control Medal, which is awarded only to companies that have been awarded the Deming Prize more than five years earlier. The criteria are the same as for the Deming Prize, only a company must score above 75 instead of the 70 for the Deming Application Prize. The final level is the Ishikawa Prize, which is given for development of new methods or systems in management and quality control. In all of these levels of recognition, the most distinctive award is the Deming Prize.

THE BALDRIGE AWARD PROCESS

The Intention of the Baldrige Award

The Malcolm Baldrige National Quality Award is an annual award to recognize U.S. companies that excel in quality management and quality achievement. The award promotes an awareness of quality as an increasingly important element in competitiveness; an understanding of the requirements for quality excellence; sharing of information on successful quality strategies; and the benefits derived from implementation of these strategies. Up to two awards may be given each year in each of three eligibility categories: manufacturing companies, service companies, and small businesses. The award examination evaluates applicants according to a set of criteria and scoring guidelines, which are included in the Application Guidelines.

The Baldrige criteria are designed to be a quality excellence standard for organizations seeking the highest level of overall quality performance and competitiveness. These criteria are reviewed and improved on an annual basis to reflect lessons learned during the evaluation process. The award is managed by the National Institute of Standards and Technology (NIST) and administered by the American Society of Quality Control (ASQC). The evaluation of applicants is conducted by a Board of Examiners nominated from the quality experts of business, professional and trade organizations, accrediting bodies, universities, and government. Members of the Board of Examiners must meet the highest standards of qualification and peer recognition. The Board of Examiners evaluates each application, considering the context of the applicant's business factors, according to the award criteria, following a prescribed evaluation process, and using an established scoring guideline. Each of these elements of the Baldrige Award process is described below.

The Effect of Business Factors

While the Baldrige Award criteria have been designed for their general application for evaluation of any company's quality system, independent of size, type of business, or market environment, it is recognized that the importance of individual business factors for a given company may influence the applicability of the items and areas to address, even for businesses of comparable size or in the same industry.

Levels of Quality Assessment

A simplified way of summarizing quality assessment is to look at it in four levels of deployment.

1. A self-assessment is undertaken by the local management. An example of this approach is a management team review of various departments. This type of assessment does not tend to be objective; however, it has the advantage of conditioning management to conducting internal reviews. Another example of this type of assessment is also the project review.
2. A company-sponsored self-assessment is conducted by assessors from external organizations. An example of this approach is a companywide survey on quality performance.[11] While this approach does improve the objectivity of the observations, it is not likely to provide the same degree of accuracy as direct observation.
3. This level of deployment uses evaluation criteria and culminates with a site visit by trained assessors (either from within the company or outside) who clarify any questionable areas of the application and verify the claims of the written application.

4. A written application is submitted to an external organization and certified, external quality professionals conduct both the written evaluation and site-visit assessment. This is the approach of all the major quality award sponsoring agencies.

Since the highest level of assessment contains more complexity than the lower levels, we will evaluate the Malcolm Baldrige National Quality Award evaluation process in detail to understand how the assessment process works.

To give appropriate consideration to these distinctions, the application requests a four-page overview, which does not count toward the page limit, that addresses key business factors that must be considered during the award evaluation process. These business factors set the context for the interpretation of the entire application and are exceptionally important. Information that is important to consider as business factors include:

- Business structure of the applicant and relationship to parent company (if a subsidiary)
  Note: Subsidiaries should also include information that shows key relationships to the parent company:
    (1) Percent of employees
    (2) Percent of sales
    (3) Types of products and services
- Size and resources of the applicant
- Types of major products and services
- Key quality requirements for products and services
- Nature of markets (local, regional, national, or international)
- Description of principal customers (consumers, other businesses, government)
- Competitive environment
- Applicant's position in the industry
- Major equipment and facilities used
- General description of the applicant's employment base, including number, type, and education level
- Importance of and types of suppliers of goods and services
- Occupational health and safety, environmental, and other regulatory considerations
- Other factors important to the applicant

The Evaluation Process

The Baldrige Award evaluation process contains four stages: review of the written application; consensus review of the written application; site-visit review; and judges' final review. Each applicant receives a feedback report describing the Board of Examiners' assessment as to the Strengths and Areas for Improvement for each examination item in the application. The feedback report states observations and evaluations, not prescriptions on how to improve the applicant's quality process. The feedback report is prepared after an application has been eliminated from further consideration at one of the four stages of review.

The first-stage review of the written application is conducted as an independent review by five or more members of the Board of Examiners. Each examination item is graded in accordance with the scoring system. The Board of Examiners takes the application at face value. They accept the facts as presented and, when questions arise, they record them for verification or clarification at the site visit. The scorebooks from each evaluation are returned to NIST/ASQC and the judges select the top-scoring applications for the consensus review. The written comments of the examiners from the first-stage review are used as the basis of the feedback report for applicants not selected for the consensus review.

The consensus review of the higher-scoring applications from the first-stage review is conducted by a team of five examiners, led by a senior examiner. Consensus is initiated by the team leader with a goal of achieving an agreed-upon scoring value for each of the examination items after the team has debated the relative merits of the applicant's approach, deployment, and results for that item. This is a particularly important step in the award process, because consensus numerical scores play a major role in determining which applicants will receive a site visit and in determining issues for review during the site visit. In addition, the written comments of the examiners from the consensus review are used as the basis of the feedback report for applicants that are not selected for site visits. Using these written comments, the senior examiner prepares a consensus report for the judges, and the judges select the top-scoring applicants for site visits.

Finalists in the award process receive a site visit from a team of six members of the Board of Examiners, led by a senior examiner. The team visits one or more sites (labs, plants, offices) of the applicant to *clarify* uncertain points in the application and to *verify* that the information presented by the applicant is correct. There are five distinct steps in the site-visit process:

- *Notification:* The panel of judges selects applicants for site visits and transmits the information to the award administrator who notifies the applicant and the appropriate members of the Board of Examiners.
- *Initial preparation:* The team leader works with the NIST observer, award administrator, team members, and the point of contact from the applicant to establish the agenda and logistics for the site visit. Members of the site visit team review evaluation materials and perform tasks as assigned by the team leader.
- *Final preparation:* The team holds a day-long preparatory meeting immediately preceding the site visit. They finalize the agenda and category assignments, review site-visit issues, and prepare the site-visit worksheet, which addresses the issues that the team will evaluate. This meeting is not held at the applicant's site.
- *Conduct of the site visit:* The actual site visit begins with an initial meeting with the applicant. During this meeting the team leader presents the agenda and objectives. After this introductory meeting, the site-visit team divides and performs the individual category assignments. The team caucuses as often as necessary to ensure that all assignments are being implemented, all issues and questions are being adequately addressed, and the schedule is being followed. When the team leader and members are satisfied that all issues have been clarified or verified, the team leader closes the site visit by holding a meeting with the appropriate applicant representatives.
- *Preparation of the site-visit report:* The site visit team completes the site-visit worksheet and a report of their findings and conclusions about each category, including the strengths and areas for improvement. The team leader reviews these worksheets for completeness and prepares a "Recommendation to the Judges" worksheet.

Following the receipt of the site-visit reports, the judges meet for the final review to verify that the Baldrige Award process was followed, review the site-visit reports, and make recommendations of the award recipients. The award administrator forwards the judges' recommendations to the secretary of Commerce for selection.

Interpretation of the Criteria

Some consulting companies have hinted that there is a hidden agenda in terms of what the judges and examiners are seeking in a "Baldrige-winning" company. But, there are no secrets. One member of the Board of Examiners has even published a book that presents his interpretation of the examination items and what the examiners evaluate.[12] The Board of Examiners is seeking a company that represents a national role model for quality based on that company's approach and deployment of its quality program as well as the results attributable to that program. The essential elements of the award criteria are described in the application guidelines. Together, the following key concepts and core concepts define the infrastructure for the requirements of the examination items:

- *Customer-driven quality:* Quality is defined by the customer. Business fundamentals such as design quality and defect or error prevention, which affect the customer, should be part of the quality system.
- *Leadership:* The senior leadership of businesses must create clear quality values and build these values into the way the company operates.
- *Continuous improvement:* Quality excellence derives from well-designed and well-executed systems and processes. Continuous improvement must be part of the management of all systems and processes. Companies need to communicate quality requirements to suppliers and distributors and work as a team to improve the performance of the entire business.
- *Fast response:* Shortening the response time of all operations and processes of the company needs to be part of the quality improvement effort.
- *Actions based on facts, data, and analysis:* Companies need to develop goals, as well as strategic and operational plans, to achieve quality leadership. Operations and decisions of the company need to be based upon facts and data.
- *Participation of all employees:* All employees must be suitably trained, developed, and involved in quality activities.

The 1991 Baldrige Award criteria are summarized in Appendix C. It is important to understand the context in which these criteria are used.

The Baldrige examination is a two-part diagnostic system (see Figure 8-2). The first part, criteria, includes the seven categories, which are divided into areas to address as well as the detailed description of these areas, called the examination items. Taken together, the criteria represent "what" is to be evaluated.

Parts	Contents
I. Criteria What is to be evaluated	The Seven Categories • Areas to address • Examination items
II. Scoring System How evaluations are made	• Approach • Deployment • Results

Figure 8-2. Baldrige Two-Part Diagnostic System

The second part of the diagnostic system, the scoring system, represents "how" evaluations are made.

The examination is nonprescriptive. While it is based on the values and key concepts described above, the examination does not prescribe the specific means (specific techniques, methodologies, or organizational structure) to demonstrate excellence. The examination emphasizes the integration of the entire quality system. The examination items represent a system of requirements. Thus, quality system integration is the result of a company establishing the linkages among the direct and indirect relationships between the examination items. A coherent quality system demonstrates how these linkages are put into practice. In the findings of this benchmarking study, the relationships among the examination items are demonstrated using an affinity diagram.[13]

Scoring Guidelines

The scoring system is based on three evaluation dimensions: approach, deployment, and results. All examination items require applicants to provide information or data relating to one or more of these dimensions. Each of the examination items is graded according to a scheme that considers the applicant's approach, deployment of that approach, and results demonstrated from that deployment. The specific interpretation of these dimensions is found in the table of scoring guidelines in Table 8-1. A list of operational definitions follows.

Approach refers to the methods an organization uses to achieve the purpose described in the examination item. The examiners consider such aspects of the approach as:

• The degree to which the approach is prevention based
• The appropriateness of the tools, techniques, and methods chosen to meet the requirements

Table 8-1. Scoring Guidelines

Score	Approach	Deployment	Results
0%	• anecdotal, no system evident	• anecdotal	• anecdotal
10-40%	• beginning of prevention basis	• some to many major areas of business	• some positive trends in areas deployed
50%	• sound, systematic prevention basis that includes evaluation/ improvement cycles	• most major areas of business • some support areas	• positive trends in most major areas • some evidence that results are caused by approach
60-90%	• sound, systematic prevention basis with evidence of refinement through evaluation/improvement cycles • good integration	• major areas of business • from some to many support areas	• good to excellent in major areas • positive trends – from some to many support areas • evidence that results are caused by approach
100%	• sound, systematic prevention basis refined through evaluation/improvement cycles • excellent integration	• major areas and support areas • all operations	• excellent (world-class) results in major areas • good to excellent in support areas • sustained results • results clearly caused by approach

- The effectiveness of the use of the tools, techniques, and methods
- The degree to which the approach is systematic, integrated, and consistently applied
- The degree to which the approach embodies effective evaluation or improvement cycles
- The degree to which the approach is based upon quantitative information that is objective, timely, and reliable
- The utilization of unique and innovative approaches, including significant and effective new adaptations of tools and techniques used in other applications or types of business

Deployment refers to the extent to which the approaches are applied to all relevant areas and activities that are either addressed or implied in the examination items. The examiners consider such aspects of the deployment as its appropriate and effective application to the following:

- All product and service characteristics

- All transactions and relationships with customers, suppliers of goods and services, and the public
- All internal processes, activities, facilities, and employees

Results refers to the outcomes, effects, and achievements that are attributable to the approach and deployment. These results are based upon the purposes addressed and implied in the examination items. The examiners consider such aspects of the results as:

- The quality levels as demonstrated and supported by evidence
- The contributions of the outcomes and effects to quality improvement
- The rate of quality improvement
- The breadth of quality improvement
- The demonstration of sustained improvement
- The significance of improvements to the company's business
- The comparison with industry and world leaders
- The company's ability to show that improvements derive from their quality practices and actions

Examiners are trained to recognize companies that score at the 50 percent level of performance using these scoring guidelines. Their training calibrates this level and, through the consensus grading process, reinforces the appreciation for excellence demonstrated by performance beyond this level. A 50 percent performance means that a company has a sound, systematic, prevention-based approach that includes ongoing improvement with evidence of integration; the approach has been deployed to most major areas of the company; and positive result trends that are caused by the approach are demonstrated in major areas.

Each of the individual examination items is scored for approach, deployment, and/or results in accordance with the method shown in Table 8-2. Notice that several of the examination items require that data be presented.

The scoring process has a built-in bias to pass strongly performing companies during the first-stage review, so that contenders whose score is above the 50 percent level will receive the consensus review. This bias exists so that no contender is blocked at the early phase of consideration. During the consensus review, the team of examiners takes exceptional care to precisely define the level of performance using the scoring guidelines. Only those companies whose performance on the consensus review clearly indicates excellence (good integration of the approach with deployment to the major areas of the business, and demonstrated good-to-excellent results with positive trends, even in support areas) will pass on to the site-visit phase.

Table 8-2. Evaluation Item Scoring Table (1991 Criteria)

Item	Approach	Deployment	Results	Data Required
1.1	✔	✔		
1.2	✔	✔		
1.3	✔	✔		
1.4	✔	✔		
2.1	✔	✔		
2.2	✔	✔		
2.3	✔	✔		
3.1	✔	✔		
3.2	✔	✔		3.2d
4.1	✔	✔		
4.2	✔	✔		4.2d
4.3	✔	✔		4.3d
4.4	✔	✔		4.4d
4.5	✔	✔		4.5d
5.1	✔	✔		
5.2	✔	✔		
5.3	✔	✔		
5.4	✔	✔		
5.5	✔	✔		
5.6	✔	✔		
5.7	✔	✔		
6.1			✔	Yes
6.2			✔	Yes
6.3			✔	Yes
7.1	✔	✔		
7.2	✔	✔		
7.3	✔	✔		
7.4	✔	✔		
7.5	✔	✔	7.5b	Yes
7.6	✔	✔		
7.7			✔	Yes
7.8			✔	Yes

Study Findings

Analysis of the 1991 Criteria for the Malcolm Baldrige National Quality Award

The award criteria are linked in Table 8-3 to critical factors for business process management and the quality tools that support them. This summary of an integrated approach for using quality tools is one product of applying the

Table 8-3. 1991 Baldrige Criteria Linked to CSFs and Enablers

Award Criteria Category	Critical Success Factors	Quality Tool Enablers
1.0 Leadership	Executive communication Management's visibility Executive involvement Public responsibility	Culture values Business vision Mission statement Company goals
2.0 Information & Analysis	Information reliability Accuracy of data Timeliness of data Information integration	Information technology Activity based costing Competitive analysis Benchmarking
3.0 Strategic Quality Planning	Goal-setting process Management review Team participation	Hoshin kanri Daily management Cross-functional teams
4.0 Human Resource Utilization	Strategic HR plan Curriculum development Employee selection Employee retention Competitive benefits Health & safety Organization structure	Quality teams Employee involvement Quality training Suggestion systems Recognition programs Gainsharing Position description Performance review Coaching/mentoring
5.0 Quality Assurance of Products & Services	Quality assurance Quality planning Quality control Quality audits Quality improvement	Quality analysis tools Design of experiments Statistical process control Variability reduction ISO 9000
6.0 Quality Results	Performance monitor Trend analysis Management review	Quality assessment Supplier quality program Competitive intelligence
7.0 Customer Satisfaction	Complaint management Service performance Rapid communication Customer knowledge • Requirements • Expectations • Aspirations Customer guarantee	Quality function deployment Customer focus groups Custor satisfaction surveys Competitive product analysis Market research Industry analysis Product warranty Product positioning

Baldrige criteria as a coherent quality system. Some critics of the Baldrige Award cannot seem to see past the cost of application and the "cottage industry" of consultants.[14] However, many valuable lessons have been learned from the application of these criteria. (See "Lessons Learned from the Baldrige

Award.") These lessons will allow American business to continue to improve its competitive position within the global marketplace.

Interrelationships Among Baldrige Criteria

The Baldrige Award criteria represents a coherent quality system with broad application for businesses. One way to indicate the integration among the examination items is to observe the interrelationships among the criteria in the following affinity diagram. An affinity diagram is a quality tool that may be used to sort a large number of themes concurrently. It groups those items that are related and identifies the primary concept that ties each group together. In Table 8-4, a slight deviation is taken. The concepts that tie the diagram together are the seven Baldrige Award categories. The groupings below them are the areas to address from the award application form. For ease of communicating, the numbers used in the diagram are from the 1991 Baldrige Award application form.

Lessons Learned From the Baldrige Award

Some of the lessons learned from the Baldrige Award are listed below using the Baldrige categories to present them as a state of quality overview:

1.0 Leadership

- Senior management recognizes that quality is a strategic business issue.
- Executives are communicating a quality vision and an accompanying value system to their employees and building it into their company culture.
- The employment market for senior quality management positions indicates that the management structure of organizations is building an infrastructure to strategically deploy quality efforts.
- Senior executives are speaking out for quality in public forums throughout America.
- Senior managers are not convinced that quality performance drives financial performance — financial measures, rather than quality measures and the need for long-term management, still drive their perception of company performance.

Table 8-4. Interrelationships Among 1991 Baldrige Award Criteria

1.0 Leadership	2.0 Information & Analysis	3.0 Strategic Quality Planning	4.0 Human Resources Utilization	5.0 QA of Products & Services	6.0 Quality Results	7.0 Customer Satisfaction

1.1
  3.1a
  3.2b,c
	2.1
	  4.3
	  4.4
	  4.5
	  6.1
	  6.2
	  6.3
	  7.7
	  7.8
		3.1
		  1.1a
		  6.1b
		  7.8a
			4.1
			  4.5b
				5.1
				  7.1a,b,c
					6.1
					  2.2a,b
					  7.1a,b
					  7.8a,c,d
						7.1
						  5.1a,c
						  6.1a
						  7.6 Note (1)

1.2			4.2
			  1.3b
			  7.2c
			  7.5b
				5.2
				  5.3c
				  5.4b
					6.2
					  1.4c
					  5.1c
					  5.2c
					  5.3b
					  5.6a,b
						7.2
						  3.2b
						  4.3a
						  4.2b
						  7.3b
						  7.5b,c

1.3
  4.2a
  7.5d
		3.2
		  1.1a
		  4.1a
		  4.3a
		  4.3c
		  5.7a,b
		  7.2d
			4.3
			  2.1a
			  3.2b
			  7.2c
				5.4
				  5.2b		

1.4	2.2
	  6.1b
				5.5	6.3
					  5.7a,b
						7.3
						  7.2d
						  7.5c

			4.4
			  2.1a
				5.6
				  6.2a
						7.4

			4.5
			  2.1a
			  4.1a
				5.7
				  3.2b
				  6.3a
						7.5
						  1.3c
						  7.2c,d
						  7.3c
						  7.6c
						  7.7b

						7.6
						  7.1b
						  7.5d

						7.7 6.1a

						7.8
						  2.1a
						  3.1b
						  6.1b

- "Management by fact" and the concept of process thinking are applied by few senior managers to their own activities.
- Cross-functional involvement in quality planning is beginning to be seen as a necessary activity.
- Planning for quality improvement is delegated to lower levels of the organization rather than to the top-management team.

2.0 Information and Analysis

- Information technology and data bases exist in most companies.
- Benchmarking and sharing of information have increased greatly as a result of their emphasis in the Baldrige criteria; however, benchmarking is often confused with industrial tourism, and few companies obtain the full value of this tool.
- Resources are required to implement long-term measurement systems for product quality monitoring and customer and employee satisfaction surveys. The economic environment has precluded some of these investments.
- Data collected are not distributed and communicated to all parties who require the processed information.

3.0 Strategic Quality Planning

- While benchmarking is becoming a more visible tool, few companies are integrating it with their strategic planning process.
- The "Six Sigma" stretch goal of Motorola has received great publicity, and many companies are considering how to improve their goal-setting capabilities.
- Companies have poor communication methods to share their strategic goals and plans; therefore, the organization is not in alignment with these goals.
- Few companies measure the effectiveness of their planning systems as a quality management practice.

4.0 Human Resource Utilization

- Team activity has greatly increased and suggestion systems have been implemented to gain more input from employees, although participation tends to be low.
- While training budgets have increased substantially, the training tends to be basic and the effectiveness of training is not directly measured.
- Employee surveys are used to assess employee morale; however, first-level management resists the empowerment of employees, perceiving it as a risk to job security.

- While recognition has increased, recognition by presenting team quality improvement results to senior management is not greatly exercised.
- Quality of work life and the ergonomic design of working conditions are not integrated into quality programs.

5.0 Quality Assurance of Products and Services

- Manufacturing is a strong area for quality — particularly for quality teams, statistical process control, just-in-time manufacturing, and supplier quality management.
- Companies are beginning to seriously use design of experiments, Taguchi methods, and Quality Function Deployment to enhance their product design and development processes.
- The specter of the ISO 9000 registration requirements of the European Economic Community has increased management's interest in basic quality assurance.
- While quality improvement is strong in manufacturing, corrective action tends to be symptomatic rather than focused on the root cause.
- Most companies are deficient in their new product development systems, especially customer listening systems to align the product design and delivery system with the voice of the customer.
- Quality audits are not rigorously conducted in many manufacturing companies and are not conducted in service companies.
- Quality efforts tend to focus on manufacturing and fail to involve service, support, and business process areas.

6.0 Quality Results

- Quality levels are improving in many industries.
- Supplier quality programs, ISO 9000, and the Baldrige Award are all tending to improve the quality of the manufacturing supplier base.
- Many companies have not identified their key business processes and therefore do not focus on their improvement.
- Product quality measurement is favored greatly over service quality measurement or customer-perceived quality performance.

7.0 Customer Satisfaction

- There is an increased focus on quick response to customers and formal complaint resolution; however, management tends to be overdependent upon complaints as a source of customer feedback.
- People in support functions are just beginning to understand the concept of the "internal" customer.
- While customer-contact people receive motivational training, they are not fully empowered to resolve issues and are reluctant to escalate the issue to the level of the individual with the authority to make the resolution.
- The process for integrating customer data with new product design and development is informal in most companies.
- Customer segmentation tends to be incomplete, not addressing all layers of customers (such as distribution channel or final customer).
- While the use of customer surveys is increasing, there is little technical understanding of the appropriate application of survey results.
- Companies change their performance measurements frequently, producing a fragmented historical data base that hinders the comparison of trends over time.
- Companies tend to believe that replacement guarantees should satisfy the customer, rather than providing preventive action.
- Rather than aggregating complaints from all sources and dealing with them as an integrated complaint management system, complaint systems are reactive and respond to formal complaints.

Differences Between the 1991 and 1992 Baldrige Award Criteria

The 1992 Malcolm Baldrige National Award criteria (Appendix G) were improved considerably from the 1991 award criteria. An increased emphasis on business performance and results was built into the criteria to more clearly link the award criteria to quality-related corporate issues such as incremental and breakthrough improvement; financial performance; and invention, innovation, and creativity.

The 1992 award criteria use the same seven-category framework as the 1991 criteria; however, the number of items was reduced from 32 to 28 and point values were adjusted to place more emphasis on results. Numerous other changes have been made to improve clarity of the criteria and strengthen the following themes in the award:

- Cycle-time reduction
- Productivity
- Overall company performance
- Work process and organization simplification and waste reduction
- Relationship between quality and other business management considerations: business planning, financial results, overall company effectiveness, innovation, and future orientation
- Alignment of requirements in plans
- Design quality and prevention
- Data aggregation, analysis, and use
- Work-force development
- Quality system integration via Category 6.0

The following list summarizes the changes in the criteria by category and is taken from the 1992 award criteria:

1. *Leadership:* The category has been reduced from four to three items. The Quality Values item (1991) has been subsumed in items 1.1 and 1.2. The importance of personal involvement of senior executive leadership has been further stressed through increased point value and greater emphasis on executives' personal use of improvement processes.

   The Management for Quality item (1992) now requires applicants to analyze their organizational structures to determine how well they support quality, cycle time, and innovation objectives. The intent of this change is to encourage users of the criteria to work toward organizations capable of speed and flexibility, maximizing value-added work.

2. *Information and Analysis:* The importance of item 2.3 has been increased and is now more clearly the "central intelligence" item within the criteria. This item serves as the analysis point for the development of company strategy and plans and for the review of company progress. Analyses carried out in item 2.3 support the dual, results-oriented goals of the award: to project key requirements for delivering ever-improving value to customers while at the same time maximizing the overall productivity and effectiveness of the delivering organization.

The item addressing Competitive Comparisons and Benchmarks now requires applicants to describe how benchmark data encourage innovation and better knowledge of processes.

3. *Strategic Quality Planning:* Item 3.1 seeks to provide a better integration of quality and performance planning into overall business planning. Planning issues such as research and development and technology leadership are now more explicitly addressed.

Together, items 3.1 and 3.2 place more emphasis on the processes used to deploy customer and company performance requirements to all company units. The importance of such deployment is discussed under quality system alignment in the 1992 award criteria.

4. *Human Resource Development and Management:* The title of this category has been changed to better reflect development and the investment in human resources, which the category seeks to balance with utilization.

More emphasis is placed on improvement of personnel practices such as recruitment and management to achieve excellence, taking into account a more diverse work force.

5. *Management of Process Quality:* The title of this category has been changed to reflect the greater emphasis on definition, management, and improvement of processes.

The category has been reduced from seven to five items. The themes of the 1991 Continuous Improvement of Processes item have been built into all items of the category. The 1991 Documentation item requirements have been included under the Quality Assessment item for 1992. Research and development work of companies with such activities can be described in one or more of three items: 5.1, 5.2, and 5.3. Product research and development is covered under 5.1; process research and development is covered under 5.2; and basic research and development is covered under 5.3. Applicants are not expected to reveal proprietary research and development activities. However, they are expected to provide information on how they use quality principles in managing research and development for greater innovation and better coupling to the company's chosen directions.

6. *Quality and Operational Results:* The title of this category has been changed to better reflect its dual purposes and the composite nature of results.

The category has been increased from three to four items. The Business Process, Operational, and Support Services Quality Results item (1991) has been divided into two items to provide better clarity and focus. The four items of this category play a central role in the award criteria and are, therefore, described in detail:

6.1 *Product and Service Quality Results:* This item calls for reporting quality levels and improvements for key product and service attributes — attributes that truly matter to the customer and to the marketplace. These attributes are derived from customer-related items ("listening posts"), which make up Category 7.0. If the attributes have been properly selected, improvements in them should show a strong positive correlation with customer and marketplace improvement indicators — captured in items 7.4 and 7.5. The correlation between quality and customer indicators is a critical management tool. It is a device for focusing on key attributes. In addition, the correlation may reveal emerging or changing market segments or changing importance of attributes.

6.2 *Company Operational Results:* This item calls for reporting performance and improvements in quality and productivity of the company. Paralleling item 6.1, which focuses on attributes that matter to the customer, item 6.2 focuses on attributes that best reflect overall company performance. Such attributes are of two types: (1) generic — common to all companies; and (2) business-specific. Generic attributes include cycle time, internal quality, and those attributes that relate to productivity, as reflected in the use of labor, materials, energy, capital, and assets. Indicators of productivity, cycle time, or internal quality should reflect overall company performance. Business or company-specific effectiveness indicators vary greatly and may include indicators such as rates of invention, environmental quality, export levels, new markets, and percent of sales from recently introduced products or services.

6.3 *Business Process and Support Service Results:* This item calls for reporting performance and improvements in quality, productivity, and effectiveness of the business processes and support services that support the principal product and service production activities. This permits a demonstration of how support units of the company link and contribute to overall improvement in company operational performance (reported in item 6.2). This item is thus a useful device in aligning support activities with the company's principal overall quality, productivity, and business objectives. Through this item, special requirements which differ from work unit to work unit and define work unit effectiveness can be set, tracked, and linked to one another.

6.4 *Supplier Quality Result:* This item calls for reporting quality levels and improvements in key indicators of supplier quality. The term "supplier" refers to external providers of products and services, "upstream" and/or "downstream" from the company. The focus should be on the most critical quality attributes from the point of view of the company — the buyer of the products and services. Trends and levels of quality should reflect the means by which they occur — via improvements by suppliers within the supply base, through changes in the selection of suppliers, or both.

7. *Customer Focus and Satisfaction:* The title of this category has been changed to better reflect its overall purposes. The category has been reduced from eight items to six. Customer Relationship Management (1992) is a composite of three items from the 1991 criteria: Customer Relationship Management; Customer Service Standards; and Complaint Resolution for Quality Improvement.

The 1991 item, Determining Customer Requirements and Expectations, is given more of a future orientation in the 1992 criteria. The new title of the item is Future Requirements and Expectations of Customers. This item (7.6) occurs last in the sequence. The first five items in the category are devoted to current and near-term customer issues.

COMPARISON OF 1991 QUALITY AND PRODUCTIVITY AWARD CRITERIA

Five major quality awards have been presented in America: the Deming Application Prize, the Malcolm Baldrige National Quality Award, the President's Award for Quality and Productivity Improvement, the George M. Low

Trophy (NASA's Productivity and Excellence Award), and the Shingo Prize for Excellence in American Manufacturing. This section of the study describes the particulars of each award and compares the various award criteria and scoring systems.

The Deming Application Prize

The Deming Prize was established in 1951 to honor the contributions of Dr. W. Edwards Deming to the quality control movement within Japan. The prize is awarded in three categories: Deming Application Prize for Division, Deming Application Prize for Small Business, and Quality Control Award for Factory. In addition, individuals who have uniquely contributed to Japan's body of knowledge about quality control and statistical methods may be awarded a Deming Prize. Any company that qualifies for the Deming Application Prize will receive it — the prize is awarded without external competition, and there is no maximum number of companies that may receive the award in a given year.

To qualify for the Deming Application Prize, top management must apply. This is called challenging the Deming Prize. The process to receive the award lasts three to five years, and the company's managers must convince the Deming Prize Committee that they are prepared for an on-site examination. The experts serve as examiners and audit the state of the quality system, paying particular attention to the use of statistical methods and using a brief set of "particulars" called the Deming Prize Application Checklist (Appendix B). To qualify for the award, a company must score 70 points or more; top management must score at least 70 points; and no unit of the company may score less than 50 points. Companies that have applied for the prize receive a report of the comments and recommendations of the Deming Prize Committee. The report contains findings about desirable and undesirable aspects of the company's quality operations and includes constructive suggestions for change.

The Malcolm Baldrige National Quality Award

The Malcolm Baldrige National Quality Award was established by President Ronald Reagan in 1987 to honor Malcolm Baldrige, the late secretary of the Department of Commerce. The Baldrige Award has three categories for application: manufacturing, service, and small business. The Baldrige Award is competitive among the annual applicants, and only two awards may be given in each category annually; however, the Board of Examiners may elect not to present an award in a particular category during a given year.

To qualify for the Baldrige Award, top management must apply. While the process to receive the award lasts one year from the time of application to the time of award announcement, it may take a company three to five years, or more, to develop a quality system that is competitive for the award. The application for the award is limited to 75 single-sided pages for the two large business categories and 50 pages for small businesses. To qualify for the award, the applicant goes through an extensive process (see the above section on the Baldrige process). To be a contender for the award, a company should be capable of scoring well above 700 points on the application. The highest score to date on the application has been in the mid-800 point range. However, the Baldrige Award is not granted solely on the competitive score. A more subjective assessment by the judges is also made to evaluate the potential for the applicant to serve as a national role model for quality improvement. Each company that applies for the Baldrige Award will receive a feedback report that describes the findings of the Board of Examiners relative to the company's strengths and areas for improvement.

The President's Award for Quality and Productivity Improvement

The President's Award for Quality and Productivity Improvement was established by President George Bush in 1988 to recognize quality and productivity improvements among agencies of the federal government. An agency becomes eligible to apply for the President's Award if one or more Quality Improvement Prototypes (QIPs) have been selected from that agency. The Quality Improvement Prototype Award is given to smaller units within an agency that have made significant improvements in quality and productivity. The criteria for these awards are contained in the *Federal TQM Handbook* (the President's Award is summarized in Appendix D). The criteria for the QIP Award are a subset of the President's Award criteria. While the President's Award may be given to two agencies annually, up to six governmental units can receive QIP Awards each year.

To qualify for the award, top management must apply; however, unlike the Baldrige Award, applications are mailed to eligible agencies by the Federal Quality Institute. Like the Baldrige Award, the President's Award cycle is one year; however, this does not indicate the amount of time that it will take a government agency to become competitive for receiving the award. The application for the award is limited to 35 single-sided pages for agencies under 20,000 employees and 60 pages for larger agencies. To qualify for the award, the applicant is evaluated by a panel of judges using scoring guidelines. Only two President's Awards have been presented to date, so information about the competitive range is not available. The guidelines for the award indicate that scores in the range of 80 to 100 percent are considered to be world class. As a measure of comparison, 40 to 60 percent scores in the award criteria categories indicate an organization with a sound, well-implemented program. As with the Baldrige Award, the score is not the sole determinant of the consideration for the President's Award. A more subjective assessment by the judges is also made to evaluate the applicant's potential to serve as a role model to government agencies for TQM implementation and quality improvement. Applicants receive an evaluation of their application by the panel of judges.

The George M. Low Trophy, NASA's Productivity and Excellence Award

The NASA Award precedes the Baldrige Award by three years. It was initially established in 1984 by James Beggs, the administrator of NASA, to honor those companies that have contributed to the success of the nation's aerospace efforts and to encourage superior quality and productivity in the aerospace industry. The award was renamed the George M. Low Trophy in 1991 in memory of an early pioneer in the development of the NASA Space Programs. The award is presented in two categories: large and small business. The award is not competitive and may be given to as many applicants as demonstrate the level of excellence required over the period of time specified.

Top management must decide to apply for the award and submits a letter of nomination with a brief statement of eligibility compliance. If selected by the Evaluation Committee to compete, the applicant then completes a 35-page application in response to the award criteria (summarized in Appendix E). The report guidelines require that data covering a three-year performance window be provided in the report. The Evaluation Committee reviews the applications and selects the finalists to receive site visits. The scoring guidelines for the NASA Award are considerably different from the Baldrige and President's Awards. The NASA scoring guidelines describe excellence as scores in the 91 to 100 percent range, and the scores of award recipients range between 800 and 900 points. All award applicants may request a debriefing to identify strengths and areas for improvement. Debriefings are conducted either face-to-face or by teleconference.

The Shingo Prize for Excellence in American Manufacturing

The Shingo Prize for Excellence in American Manufacturing was established in 1988 to honor Shigeo Shingo who, with Taiichi Ohno, was the cocreator of the revolutionary manufacturing techniques, methods, and processes that make up the Toyota production system. This prize recognizes companies and plants in the United States that have demonstrated outstanding achievements in manufacturing processes, quality, productivity enhancement, and customer satisfaction.

The Shingo Prize is awarded in two categories, large and small businesses, and only two awards may be given in each category. In addition, individuals who conduct professional research (whether in industry, academia, or consulting) in the field of manufacturing excellence may submit a paper for consideration in a competition for a Shingo Research Prize. The Research Prize has three categories: professional, graduate students, and undergraduate students. Up to three awards may be given annually in each category.

To qualify for the Shingo Prize, top management must apply. The Shingo Prize follows the same examination process as the Baldrige Award. The first stage compares the written application to the Prize Achievement Criteria (Appendix F). The Board of Examiners makes its award recommendations to the Shingo Prize Council following site visits to the finalists. The decisions of the Prize Council are final. Companies that have applied for the prize receive a report citing notable accomplishments and opportunities for possible improvement within their manufacturing systems.

Comparison of Award Criteria

These five awards have similarities in the way that they recognize improvement in company performance in the areas of quality and productivity. All of these awards recognize the need for management attention (Baldrige Category 1.0), teamwork and empowerment (Baldrige Category 4.0), and quality assurance (Baldrige Category 5.0), which produces results. The NASA Award and the Shingo Prize do not specifically address information and analysis (Baldrige Category 2.0) or strategic quality planning (Baldrige Category 3.0).

The Deming Prize Application Checklist does not specifically address customer satisfaction (Baldrige Category 7.0). One interesting observation from this study is that the Shingo Prize, with only slight changes, could apply equally well to a service company.[15]

Table 8-5 references each of the various award criteria to the seven Baldrige Award criteria and provides an assessment of the strength of the criteria for that category. Note that the most complete award, relative to the Baldrige, is the President's Award. This is not surprising since the President's Award was developed following the Baldrige Award.

Table 8-5. Comparison of Quality Award Evaluation Criteria

Categories	Deming Prize	MBNQA	President's Award	NASA Award	Shingo Prize
Leadership	1, 2 ◯	1 +	1 +	2.1 ◯	IA +
Information & Analysis	4 ◯	2 +	6 ◯		
Strategic Quality Planning	10 ◯	3 +	2 +		
Human Resource Utilization	3 ◯	4 +	4,5 +	2.2 +	IB +
Quality Assurance of Products and Services	5, 6, 7, 8 +	5 ◯	7 ◯	1.2 ◯	IC, IIIB +
Quality Results	9 +	6 ◯	8 ◯	1.3 ◯	IIIA, B +
Customer Satisfaction		7 +	3 +	1.1 ◯	IC, IIIC +

Numbers identify categories in respective awards.

◯ = Area for Improvement   + = Adequately Covered

The Shingo Prize achievement criteria are strong relative to the Baldrige Award, but they are not as complete. The NASA Award criteria are not as complete, nor as robust, as the Baldrige criteria, with the exception of the human resources area (section 2.2 in the NASA criteria). The Deming Prize particulars are stronger than the Baldrige in categories 5.0 and 6.0, but not as complete in all of the other areas. All of the Baldrige categories are addressed by the Deming Prize particulars except for category 7.0 (Customer Satisfaction). Category 5.0 was judged as weak in the Baldrige since it does not have a strong focus on cycle time and waste reduction. (Companies that pursue ISO 9000 certification or integrate ISO 9000 with the Baldrige criteria will eliminate this perceived area for improvement.) Category 6.0 was judged as weak in the Baldrige since it does not provide a strong assessment of business results. (Note that this area was changed significantly in the 1992 Baldrige Award criteria.)

Comparison of Category Weighting

The quality system implicit in a quality award should exhibit the characteristics of both customer satisfaction and continuous improvement. Customer satisfaction means that the applicants for the award feel that they have been accurately and fairly judged and that the assessment provides them with value in terms of increased self-knowledge of their quality system's strengths and areas for improvement. Continuous improvement means that interpretation of the criteria changes and of the scores achieved from year to year are difficult to compare. Scoring an application is probably the most emotional aspect of the assessment process. The first aspect of scoring is the weighting of the categories. Table 8-6 shows an assessment of the various award systems and their approach to weighting their categories. This was done by using the categories normalized to the Baldrige criteria from the previous section.

Note that the Deming Prize is the only award that is prescriptive and has a fixed criteria definition. The Deming categories are not formally weighted; however, many areas of the company are graded and the entire grade sheet is used in each area. The purpose of each award is reflected in how the categories are weighted. (Most notably, in the Shingo Prize, applicants can score a maximum of 500 points in the single category of manufacturing improvement. Likewise, the Deming Prize gives 400 points in process control, and the Baldrige gives 300 points in customer satisfaction.) The weighting of these categories is used to reflect the value system of the award as well as the behavior desired in the successful applicants.

Comparison of Award Scoring Systems

Interestingly, neither the Deming Application Prize nor the Shingo Prize has a formal scoring system. The Baldrige scoring system was described earlier.

Table 8-6. Comparison of Category Weighting

Award:		Deming Prize	MBNQA	President's Award	NASA Award	Shingo Prize
Scoring Basis:		Prescriptive	Non-prescriptive	Non-prescriptive	Non-prescriptive	Non-prescriptive
Criteria Definition Stability:		Fixed	Continuously Improving	Continuously Improving	Continuously Improving	Continuously Improving
Point Maximum:		100	1000	200	1000	100%
Categories Weighted:		No	Yes	Yes	Yes	Yes
Weighting Relative Category	1	200	100	100	220	100
	2	100	70	75	0	0
	3	100	60	75	0	0
	4	100	150	150	180	100
	5	400	140	150	250	500
	6	100	180	250	120	200
	7	0	300	200	230	100

A matrix is included in the application guidelines to show how the examiners are to assign scores to particular items depending on the approach/deployment/results for that particular examination item. The scoring system for the President's Award is so specific in its definitions of behaviors that it borders on a prescriptive approach. The NASA scoring guidelines are skewed to the high side since 70 to 80 percent of the points in a category can be obtained by "gradual continual improvement." The NASA Award is unique in that it uses a specific duration for the system's being in place, percent of deployment, resource allocation levels for quality program, and the degree of planning integration as indicators of the scoring. The NASA Award has the most complex of the scoring systems.

ANALYSIS OF ALTERNATIVE APPROACHES TO INTERNAL ASSESSMENT

The 23 companies studied in this analysis could be grouped into four categories based on their approach to the administration of the assessment criteria. These categories include self-assessment only, self-assessment plus MBNQA assessment, MBNQA assessment, and customized internal assessment program. These four categories and the number of companies that took each approach are shown below:

1. *Self-assessment (5 companies)*
   This class of company uses a survey or set of forms to conduct their internal Baldrige assessment.

2. *Self-assessment plus MBNQA assessment (1 company)*
   This company uses the self-assessment to screen divisions before they apply for an internal award.

3. *MBNQA criteria used for internal assessment (9 companies)*
   These companies followed the Baldrige examination process and used the Baldrige criteria.

4. *Company-developed customized approach (8 companies)*
   These companies adapted the MBNQA criteria to their company's culture. These companies included Control Data Corporation, Hewlett-Packard, IBM Europe, Intel, Procter & Gamble, Westinghouse, Whirlpool, and Xerox.

Although two of the companies offering standard MBNQA-clone company awards had multiple award levels (e.g., bronze, silver, and gold), there was not much originality in the development of these awards. Most of the unique applications for internal assessment are found in the custom category. The unique items in these assessment programs will be described in the next sections. In addition, the single company that combined self-assessment with the MBNQA evaluation approach will be discussed. Since the American practice of TQC diagnostic internal assessment goes back only about eight years — Westinghouse having the earliest internal assessment program — this is a relatively new practice. Other than a few of the "quality regulars," there has been little in-depth revision of the Baldrige criteria. Since this is the case, there is too little data to call a practice "best." Hence, the unique practices will be considered interesting processes or at least different approaches.

Company A

This company uses a self-assessment survey by all of the divisions as a screening mechanism to determine finalists for its internal award program.

These finalists then prepare an application and go through an MBNQA process to compete for the companywide award.

Company B

This company does not use the Baldrige criteria at all, but uses two radar diagrams to display its management and product quality profiles. The management profile has eight dimensions: planning, recognition, participation, trust, cooperation, environmental, people management, and acceptance of new ideas. On the product profile they have six dimensions: price, service, reliability, functionality, user friendliness, and documentation. A cross-functional management team reviews the application of these dimensions within the departments.

Company C

This company has customized the Baldrige categories to its own cultural norms to define worldwide excellence: substituting fact-based management for information and analysis; strategic planning for strategic quality planning; people for human resource utilization; quality of processes and products for quality assurance of products and services; and measurement and results for quality results. The leadership and customer satisfaction categories stayed the same. The areas to address under each category have been defined in terms of the company's programs and culture. Otherwise, this company follows the MBNQA process.

Company D

This company translated the seven Baldrige categories into five categories, which they call the five areas of quality management: planning process, customer focus, improvement cycle, process management, and total participation. Each of these different categories was uniquely defined for the company's quality program and culture. The MBNQA scoring system is used for the evaluation, and results are displayed using a radar diagram with these five categories comprising an operating unit's quality profile.

Company E

This company merged the MBNQA criteria with ISO 9000 and its own long-standing "reliability essentials" program to create a composite set of evaluation criteria.

Company F

This company uses a twelve-category evaluation criterion, called the conditions for excellence, for its internal assessment process: customer orientation, participation, development, motivation, products and services, processes and procedures, information, suppliers, culture, planning, communications, and accountability. The company has also changed the weighting system for the categories and uses a unique scoring system. Another twist this company puts on the Baldrige process is the use of external examiners and judges as their assessors. Otherwise, their method follows the Baldrige process.

Company G

This company uses the Baldrige process to determine eligibility for its internal company award. After a division has scored 500 points on the written first-stage application, then they are eligible for a site visit where they are evaluated on the six dimensions of the company's values: results orientation, risk taking, discipline, customer satisfaction, quality, and being a great place to work. The administration processes follow those of the Baldrige Award.

Company H

This company has not decided to start an award process, but has challenged each operating unit to use the Baldrige criteria to achieve a "Baldrige certification," which occurs when they score over 750 points as verified by a one-day site visit from a team of examiners. This challenge is not too burdensome from the paperwork viewpoint since the site visit is principally oral. This company basically uses a Deming scoring system with the Baldrige criteria.

Company I

This company imposes a 20-page limit on applicants and applies unique award criteria tied to its operational definition of TQM. Eligibility for the award includes business units, divisions, teams, and individuals. Three questions are evaluated in the application: why was the problem chosen, how was the problem approached, and what results were obtained and how significant were they. Each of these three questions is scored according to the contribution of innovation, leadership, product, and service.

Biggest Area for Improvement

The biggest area for improvement in the internal assessment area is the scoring process used by the internal examiners. In one company's training of internal examiners they found point spreads in scoring to be greater than 400 points at the examination item level, which implies that the examiners needed more training to calibrate their observation skills.

ISO 9000 REQUIREMENTS

Another factor affecting the quality systems for many companies is ISO 9000, the international quality standard. ISO 9000 requires its own assessment system, which, as observed above in the Company E approach to using the Baldrige Award criteria for internal assessment, needs to be considered in an internal assessment system.

In 1992 the European Community began its economic union into a common market. One feature of this union is the selection of a single standard of assurance that a product was produced in a quality-controlled production process. This standard, ISO 9000, is similar to a contract between a purchaser and a supplier. The name ISO stands for the International Standards Organization. The compliance of an individual company to this standard is monitored by an independent third party such as the British Standards Institution or Underwriters Laboratory. As a matter of business prudence, companies will need to comply with ISO 9000 to remain competitive in the common market.

ISO 9000 is a series of international standards that apply in the relationship between purchasers and suppliers. ISO 9000 identifies the basic disciplines of a manufacturer's quality system and specifies practical procedures and approaches to ensure that products and services meet customers' requirements. ISO 9000 describes three approaches to implementing a quality system. The appropriate standard depends on the business model of your company.

- *ISO 9001:* Applies to a firm that develops customer-specified or custom products or services.
- *ISO 9002:* Applies to a firm that manufactures products or provides services to a published specification or fixed product listing.
- *ISO 9003:* Applies to a firm that assures product or service quality only at final inspection and test.

In addition to these three instructions, ISO 9004 provides criteria to more clearly link the award criteria to quality-related corporate issues such as incremental and breakthrough improvement, financial performance, invention, innovation, and creativity.

CONCLUSION

This study has evaluated internal assessment systems from several different perspectives. It has attempted to provide a basis for companies to determine their most appropriate approach to internal quality assessment. Each organization, in the final analysis, must determine its own quality requirements and ways to address, most appropriately, the needs of its customers.

NOTES

1. Noriaki Kano, Hideaki Tanaka, and Yukio Yamaga, "The TQC Activity of Deming Prize Recipients and Its Economic Impact," *Quality*, April 1, 1983 (Tokyo, JUSE Press).
2. David A. Garvin, "How the Baldrige Award Really Works," *Harvard Business Review*, November–December 1991, p. 80.
3. General Accounting Office, GAO NSIAD 91-190, *Management Practices – U.S. Companies Improve Performance through Quality Efforts*, May 1990.
4. American Productivity & Quality Center, *Executive Summary: The State of Benchmarking*, January 3, 1992. Another study by the Manufacturers' Al-

liance for Productivity and Innovation (MAPI) conducted a similar survey to determine, based on the Baldrige criteria, current practices for quality improvement. Of the 131 companies surveyed, all reported improvement in the quality of their goods and services. Copies of the MAPI report, *Survey on Quality — Using the Malcolm Baldrige Criteria to Determine the State of the Art*, Economic Report 205, may be obtained by calling MAPI at (202) 331-8430.

5. American Productivity & Quality Center, *Assessing Your Organization: Do's, Don'ts, and Maybe's*, 1990. Appendix B of that document contains a quick quality assessment tool for evaluating the current state of your quality program.

6. ANSI/ASQC Standard Q1 – 1986, *Generic Guidelines for Auditing of Quality Systems*.

7. Several books are available that address the various aspects of quality audits: Dennis R. Arter, *Quality Audits for Improved Performance*, Milwaukee, ASQC Quality Press, 1989; Charles A. Mills, *The Quality Audit: A Management Evaluation Tool*, New York, McGraw-Hill, 1989; Charles B. Robinson, editor, *How to Plan an Audit*, Milwaukee, ASQC Quality Press, 1987; Alan J. Sayle, *Management Audits: The Assessment of Quality Management Systems*, Milwaukee, ASQC Quality Press, 1988; and Walter Willborn, *Audit Standards — A Comparative Analysis*, Milwaukee, ASQC, 1987. In addition, the January 1987 issue of *Quality Progress* was dedicated as a special issue on quality auditing.

8. An extreme example of management's lack of awareness of their responsibility for quality was reported in the October 17, 1989, edition of the *Wall Street Journal* on page A 10. The headline reads: "18 Chinese Managers Executed for Shoddy Product Quality." The story describes how 18 managers at the Chien Bien Refrigerator Factory were executed for ignoring quality and forcing shoddy work. Customers were waiting up to five years for their refrigerators and then were outraged when the delivered refrigerators did not operate. The managers' execution was witnessed by the 500 plant workers.

9. Kaoru Shimoyamada, "The President's Audit: QC Audits at Komatsu," *Quality Progress*, January 1987, pp. 44-49.

10. More detail on the Presidential Audit is contained in Kaoru Ishikawa, "The Quality Control Audit," *Quality Progress*, January 1987, pp. 39-43 and Kaoru Ishikawa, *What Is Total Quality Control*, Englewood Cliffs, NJ, Prentice-Hall, 1985, pp. 185-196.

11. Several examples of this type of assessment are available. One is included as Appendix A of the APQC report cited in footnote 5. Others include: Mark

Graham Brown, "Measuring Your Company Against the Baldrige Criteria," *The Journal for Quality and Participation*, June 1991; The National Quality Survey, an instrument of The Benchmark Partners, Inc. in Oak Brook, Illinois (phone [800] 366-7448); The Total Quality Communications Audit by Skutski & Associates, Inc. of Pittsburgh (phone [412] 281-5656).

12. Mark Graham Brown, *Baldrige Award Winning Quality: How to Interpret the Malcolm Baldrige Award Criteria*, Milwaukee, ASQC Quality Press, 1991.

13. Michael Brassard, *The Memory Jogger Plus*, Methuen, MA, GOAL/QPC, 1989, pp. 17-39. An affinity diagram is a tool to organize large groups of data into natural groupings that indicate interrelationships. Details of this method and quality management tools are provided in this book.

14. Patrick Houston, "Dubious Achievement?" *Business Month*, July 1990, pp. 40-44.

15. Richard B. Chase and David A. Garvin, "The Service Factory," *Harvard Business Review*, July-August 1989, pp. 61-69. This article shows some of the parallels between manufacturing and service businesses that could be used to make the Shingo Prize into a broader award for "waste management."

Section 9
A Bibliography of
Benchmarking Literature

- Books
- Reports
- Articles

The Center's in-house collection of literature was used as the base for this bibliography. Additional sources were researched to verify and to supplement the base list. Sources referenced include "More About Benchmarking," a supplement to *Commitment-Plus* (QPMA newsletter), August 1991; "Benchmarking, The IBM-Rochester Way"; "Readings on the Subject of Benchmarking" by Greg Watson; "Benchmarking Bibliography" from Mike Majcher (Xerox Corporation); and numerous articles brought to our attention by APQC chairman C. Jackson Grayson.

The bibliography citations are divided into three categories: books, reports, and articles. Where possible, information about availability is indicated. Asterisks in the book section indicate works related to TQM that may be useful to benchmarkers. In the article section, "Reference #" refers to APQC's identifier in the research collection.

BOOKS

Akao, Yoji, ed. *Hoshin Kanri: Policy Deployment for Successful TQM*. Cambridge: Productivity Press, 1991, 207 pages.*

Benchmarking information can be of significant use in a company's strategic planning process. *Hoshin kanri* is a strategic planning process that has been used in Japan for strategic-direction setting. Akao has edited a collection of papers that describe the various aspects of this system's approach to managing strategic change in critical business processes. Benchmarking is a process for assuring that the goals set as strategic business targets are achievable and will lead to competitive performance.

Alreck, Pamela, and Settle, Robert B. *The Survey Research Handbook*. Homewood, IL: Richard D. Irwin, 1985, 429 pages.

This book provides a foundation for conducting surveys of potential benchmark target companies to determine relative performance.

Arter, Dennis R. *Quality Audits for Improved Performance*. Milwaukee: ASQC Quality Press, 1989.*

Balm, Gerald J. *Benchmarking: A Practitioner's Guide for Becoming and Staying Best of the Best*. Schaumburg, IL: QPMA Press, 1992, 178 pp.

An executive from IBM Rochester "builds upon Camp's foundation by adding some things learned in the year since Camp's book was written — and the perspectives from another long-time benchmarking company, IBM." The author also emphasizes sound development of planning and measurement systems that are needed for operations and support management long after the current wave of a benchmarking project is completed. Legitimacy is given to several types of benchmarking (internal, competitive, functional, generic, and consultant-based) with comments on the advantages of each. Though quite redundant to Camp's classic, many new readers will find this book more practical and easier to use as a guide.

Band, William. *Creating Value for Customers: Designing & Implementing a Total Corporate Strategy*. New York: John Wiley & Sons, 1991.*

Brassard, Michael. *The Memory Jogger Plus*. Methuen, MA: GOAL/QPC, 1989, 306 pages. (Available from APQC.)*

Details of quality management and planning tools are provided in this book.

Brown, Mark G. *Baldrige Award Winning Quality: How to Interpret the Malcolm Baldrige Award Criteria*. Milwaukee: ASQC Quality Press, 1991, 42 pages. (Available from APQC.)*

This book is an in-depth review of the 1991 Baldrige criteria. Each category is broken down by areas to address with key indicators or evaluation factors and details what the Baldrige examiners are looking for when performing their assessment. Brown also describes the process a firm should take in setting out to complete a quality audit and outlines a typical application process.

Camp, Robert C. *Benchmarking: The Search for Industry Best Practices that Lead to Superior Performance*. Milwaukee: ASQC Quality Press, 1989, 299 pages. (Available from APQC.)

Camp's book is still the only source that covers the whole spectrum of benchmarking topics. This book is the single best overview on the subject.

Emory, C. William. *Business Research Methods*. Third ed., Homewood, IL: Richard D. Irwin, 1985, 760 pages.

Emory provides a basic description of research methods for the "search" phase of benchmarking, which seeks to discover what information is available about the companies you have targeted for study.

Fuld, Leonard M. *Competitor Intelligence: How to Get It — How to Use It*. New York: John Wiley & Sons, 1985, 477 pages.

Fuld has written the basic text on secondary research for competitive analysis. His information sources are also applicable for benchmarking.

Garvin, David A. *Managing Quality: The Strategic and Competitive Edge*. New York: The Free Press, 1987, 319 pages.*

Harrington, H. James. *Business Process Improvement*. New York: McGraw-Hill, 1991, 274 pages.

This book is a fundamental reference for process benchmarking since it provides one of the best approaches to process improvement, the desired result from process benchmarking. It establishes the context for benchmarking. The five phases of business process improvement are organizing for improvement, understanding the process, streamlining, measurement and control, and continuous improvement. The process of benchmarking is a necessary aspect of the measurement and control phase of business process improvement.

Jacobson, Gary, and Hillkirk, John. *Xerox: American Samurai*. New York: Macmillan, 1986.

Jacobson and Hillkirk relate the case study of Xerox and its use of benchmarking to arrive at the state of *dantotsu*, or best of the best.

Mills, Charles A. *The Quality Audit: A Management Evaluation Tool*. New York: McGraw-Hill, 1989, 309 pages.*

Knowledge of internal processes is essential to good benchmarking. One way to obtain an understanding of the current status of an organization's internal processes is to perform an audit or internal assessment by management. This book provides a look at this process from three points of view: the client of the audit, the organization being audited, and the auditor. It provides a good summary of this process.

Porter, Michael. *Competition in Global Industries*. Boston: Harvard Business School Press, 1986.

Porter edited this book of articles on the aspects of global competition. The book analyzes the strategic rationale and risks behind joint ventures, strategic alliances, and other international linkages between companies. This book highlights the organizational challenges involved in implementing global strategies and provides good insights into how to implement global strategies.

Porter, Michael. *Competitive Advantage: Creating and Sustaining Superior Performance*. New York: Free Press, 1985, 557 pages.

This book builds upon Porter's first book and addresses how a firm can create and sustain a competitive advantage in its industry through the development of a broad strategy based on analysis of the value chain. This book provides good insights into the means that diversified firms use to create value among their interrelated business units.

Porter, Michael. *The Competitive Advantage of Nations*. New York: Free Press, 1990, 855 pages.

Porter extends his work to focus on the concept of competitive advantage in international economics. His research identifies the fundamental determinants of national competitive advantage in a particular industry, and how this forms a competitive system for national economies.

Porter, Michael. *Competitive Strategy: Techniques for Analyzing Industries and Competitors*. New York: Free Press, 1980.

Porter examines the basic competitive strategies for coping with industry structure: cost, leadership, differentiation, and focus. He describes the functions of a competitor intelligence system and the application of this system to industry analysis. This book is a classic in business management.

Reich, Robert B. *The Work of Nations: Preparing Ourselves for 21st Century Capitalism*. New York: Alfred A. Knopf, 1991.*

Reich describes the challenging forces in the globalization of the international economic system and presents an analysis of what nations must do if their citizens are to enjoy improved living conditions in the twenty-first century. Two key observations Reich makes are the growing irrelevance of corporate nationality and the shift from volume-based to value-based production. Reich calls for a national recommitment to productivity and competitiveness for all of the nations' citizens.

Robinson, Charles B., ed. *How to Plan an Audit*. Milwaukee: ASQC Quality Press, 1987, 39 pages.*

Rummler, Geary A., and Brache, Alan P. *Improving Performance: How to Manage the White Space on the Organization Chart*. San Francisco: Jossey-Bass, 1990, 227 pages.*

This book describes organizations as adaptive systems and delineates three levels of performance that can be measured and improved: the organizational level, the process level, and the job-performance level. Rummler and Brache observe that before performance can be managed, clear expectations for that performance must be established and communicated. They present an approach to performance measurement that is linked to strategy and reflects the improvements desired in the processes.

Russell, J.P. *Quality Management Benchmark Assessment*. Milwaukee: ASQC Quality Press, 1991, 136 pages.*

This is a workbook for evaluating an organization's quality processes compared to both ISO 9000 and Malcolm Baldrige standards.

Sayle, Alan J. *Management Audits: The Assessment of Quality Management Systems*. Milwaukee: ASQC Quality Press, 1988, 400 pages.*

This book describes quality audit processes used to identify problems in business processes. One interesting chapter deals with the President's audit, which is a key tool for involving the senior management team in assessing the organization's implementation of strategic plans.

Scholtes, Peter R. *The Team Handbook: How to Use Teams to Improve Quality*. Madison, WI: Joiner Associates, 1988, 296 pages.*

Spendolini, Michael J., *The Benchmarking Book*. New York: Amacom, 1992, 224 pages.

This book provides a synthesis of lessons learned from pioneering benchmarking companies such as Xerox, AT&T, Motorola, IBM, DEC, DuPont, and Boeing. Included is a basic model showing steps needed to establish a benchmarking program.

Watson, Greg. *The Benchmarking Workbook: Adapting Best Practices for Performance Improvement*. Cambridge: Productivity Press, 1992.

This workbook provides a guide for facilitating a team through a benchmarking study. It includes forms for capturing data and a case study to help stimulate the team's project. The benchmarking workbook is written as a "user-friendly" guide to benchmarking and explains the process for benchmarking in a way that novices can appreciate. While this workbook will not make readers into benchmarking experts, it will allow them to successfully complete their first benchmarking study.

Willborn, Walter. *Audit Standards — A Comparative Analysis*. Milwaukee: ASQC Quality Press, 1987, 58 pages.*

REPORTS

The following reports are available through the American Productivity & Quality Center and the International Benchmarking Clearinghouse:

"Assessing Your Organization: *Do's, Don'ts, and Maybe's*." American Productivity & Quality Center, Houston, October 1990, 27 pages.

Byron, James and Vitalo, Raphael L. "Quality Improvement Through Exemplar-Based Productivity Analysis." Brief 82, American Productivity & Quality Center, Houston, March 1991, 8 pages.

"A Comparative Study of Internal Assessment: Using the Malcolm Baldrige National Quality Award Criteria for Measuring Quality Progress." American Productivity & Quality Center, Houston, 1992, 40 pages.

"Profiles in Excellence: A Retrospective Look at the Malcolm Baldrige National Quality Award's First Year." American Productivity & Quality Center, Houston, October 1989, 74 pages.

"Surveying Industry's Benchmarking Practices: Executive Summary." American Productivity & Quality Center, Houston, 1992, 14 pages.

Thor, Carl. "Conducting an Industry-Level Benchmarking Study." Notebook, Vol. 7, No. 6, American Productivity & Quality Center, Houston, June 1991, 4 pages.

The following reports are available for purchase from individual suppliers as indicated:

"Beating the Competition: A Practical Guide to Benchmarking." Kaiser Associates, Inc., Vienna, VA, 1988, 176 pages. Available from Kaiser Associates, 703-827-9400.

"Benchmarking." GOAL/QPC Research Committee 1991 Research Report No. 91-01, GOAL/QPC, Methuen, MA, 1991, 20 pages. Available from GOAL/QPC, Phone: 508-685-3900, FAX: 508-685-6151.

"Benchmarking for Continuous Improvement." DuPont Corporation, Wilmington, DE, 1990, 30 pages.

"Benchmarking for Quality Improvement." Xerox Report 700P06130, Xerox Corporation, Stamford, CT, 1989, 88 pages.

"Best Practices: How to Avoid Surprises in the World's Most Complicated Technical Process, The Transition from Development to Production." Best Manufacturing Practices Program, Department of the Navy, Washington, DC, 1986, 276 pages, NAVSO P-6071. Available from the Superintendent of Documents, U.S. Government Printing Office, Washington, DC, or BMP Program Office, 703-602-2128.

"A Hands-On Guide to Competitive Benchmarking: The Path to Continuous Quality and Productivity Improvement." The Verity Consulting Group, Inc., Los Angeles, 1991, 137 pages. Available form the Verity Consulting Group, 213-389-9700.

Harrington, James H. "Benchmarking." Technical Report TR90.009HJH, Ernst & Young, Los Gatos, CA, 1990, 41 pages.

"Human Resource Effectiveness Report." Saratoga Institute, Inc., Saratoga, CA, 1990, 375 pages. Available from Saratoga Institute, 408-366-7900.

"International Quality Study: The Definitive Study of the Best International Quality Management Practices." American Quality Foundation, New York, and Ernst & Young, Cleveland, 1991, 51 pages. Available through American Quality Foundation, 212-724-3170 or Ernst & Young, 216-861-5000.

"Leadership Through Quality Training Programs: Concepts of Quality Manual." Xerox Corporation, Stamford, CT, 1987, 37 pages. Available through Department of Commerce, National Technical Information Service, Springfield, VA, Report #PB91-780080.

"Leadership Through Quality Training Programs: Employee Involvement Readings – Part I: Implementing Competitive Benchmarking, Employee Involvement and Recognition." Xerox Corporation, Stamford, CT, 1987, 74 pages. Available through Department of Commerce, National Technical Information Service, Springfield, VA, Report #PB91-780056.

"Leadership Through Quality Training Programs: Employee Involvement Readings – Part II: Implementing Competitive Benchmarking, Employee Involvement and Recognition." Xerox Corporation, Stamford, CT, 1987, 101 pages. Available through Department of Commerce, National Technical Information Service, Springfield, VA, Report #PB91-780064.

"Leadership Through Quality Training Programs: Problem Solving Users Manual." Xerox Corporation, Stamford, CT, 1987, 114 pages. Available through Department of Commerce, National Technical Information Service, Springfield, VA, Report #PB91-780098.

"Leadership Through Quality Training Programs: Quality Improvement Process Workbook." Xerox Corporation, Stamford, CT, 1987, 71 pages. Available through Department of Commerce, National Technical Information Service, Springfield, VA, Report #PB91-780072.

"Management Practices: U.S. Companies Improve Performance Through Quality Efforts." GAO / NSIAD-91-190, U.S. General Accounting Office, May 1991, 42 pages. Available from U.S. GAO, 202-275-6241.

"Survey on Quality: Using the Malcolm Baldrige Criteria to Determine the State of the Art." Economic Report 205, Manufacturers' Alliance for Productivity and Innovation, Washington, DC, 1991, 33 pages. Available from MAPI, 202-331-8430.

ARTICLES

Aiki, Shigeo, "Aisin Envisions its Path to Success." *Quality Progress*, March 1992, pp. 83-87. (Reference #12325)

Albin, John T. "Competing in a Global Market." *APICS — The Performance Advantage*, January 1992, pp. 29-32. (Reference #12803)

Allaire, Paul A. "Quality: Where It Has Been and Where It Is Going." *Journal for Quality and Participation*, March 1991, pp. 64-66. (Reference #9424)

Alster, Norm. "An American Original Beats Back the Copycats." *Electronic Business*, October 1, 1987, pp. 52-58. (Reference #1777)

Altany, David. "Benchmarkers Unite: Clearinghouse Provides Needed Networking Opportunities." *Industry Week*, February 3, 1992, p. 25. (Reference #12301)

Altany, David. "Copycats." *Industry Week*, November 5, 1990, pp. 11-18. (Reference #4995)

Good introduction to the benchmarking process with a handy list of companies considered best-in-class in 15 functions from automated inventory control to warehousing and distribution.

Altany, David. "Share and Share Alike." *Industry Week*, July 15, 1991, pp. 12-17. (Reference #11370)

Nothing very "new" in this article, but it is a good overall roundup for those just beginning benchmarking.

"Baking Industry Productivity." Prepared by American Productivity Center, April 12, 1983, pp. 1-11. (Reference #3160)

Band, William. "Benchmark Your Performance for Continuous Improvement." *Sales & Marketing Management in Canada*, May 1990, pp. 36-38. (Reference #11840)

Barks, Joseph V. "Distribution Costs: A Hard Road Back." *Distribution's Logistics Annual Report*, July 1990, pp. 30-35. (Reference #11345)

Bearse, Peter J. "Improving Productivity Through Interfirm Comparisons." Peter Bearse Associates, May 1, 1983, 48 pages. (Reference #6443)

Bemowski, Karen, "The Benchmarking Bandwagon." *Quality Progress*, January 1991, pp. 19-24. (Reference #7838)

"Benchmarking, The IBM-Rochester Way." Commitment Plus, Newsletter of the Quality & Productivity Management Association, August 1991, pp. 1-4. (Reference #11841)

"Benchmarking — Presented to Harris Corporation." Kaiser Associates, Inc., October 17, 1990, 121 pages. (Reference #11708)

"Benchmarking Legal / Ethical Issues." Texas Instruments, May 24, 1991, 11 pages. (Reference #11509)

"Benchmarking: Up-Front Preparation and Strategic Perspective Lead to Benchmarking Success." Productivity, Newsletter from Productivity, Inc., September 1991, pp. 10-12. (Reference #11842)

Bemolak, Imre. "Productivity Improvement Through Comparative Analysis." AIIE 1978 Spring Annual Conference, May 23-26, 1978, pp. 185-191. (Reference #3309)

Betts, Peter J., and Baum, Neil. "Borrowing the Disney Magic." *Healthcare Forum Journal*, Jan./Feb. 1992, pp. 61-63. (Reference #12584)

Betzig, Robert J., and Fleming, Laura K. "Laying the Groundwork." *The TQM Magazine*, Vol. 2, No. 3, July/August 1992, pp. 152-154. (Reference #12978)

Biesada, Alexandra. "Benchmarking." *Financial World*. September 17, 1991, pp. 28-47. (Reference #11843)

Biesada, Alexandra. "The Second Opinion." *Financial World*, December 10, 1991, pp. 88, 90. (Reference #11942)

Blackburn, Joseph D., and Zahorik, Anthony J. "A Tale of Two Industries: Machine Tools and Plastic Injection Molding." Target, Summer 1991, pp. 13-21. (Reference #11528)

Brown, Mark Graham, "Measuring Your Company Against the Baldrige Criteria." *Journal for Quality and Participation*, June 1991, pp. 82-88. (Reference #11844)

Buderi, Robert. "The Brakes Go on in R&D." *Business Week*, July 1, 1991, pp. 24 - 26. (Reference #11750)

"The Business Week 1000: The Top 1000 U.S. Companies Ranked by Industry." *Business Week*, April 13, 1990, pp. 217-234. (Reference #11219)

Camp, Robert C. "Benchmarking: The Search for Industry Best Practices that Lead to Superior Performance. Part I: Benchmarking Defined." *Quality Progress*, January 1989, pp. 61-68. (Reference #11847)

Camp, Robert C. "Benchmarking: The Search for Industry Best Practices that Lead to Superior Performance. Part II: Key Process Steps." *Quality Progress*, January 1989, pp. 70-75. (Reference #11845)

Camp, Robert C. "Benchmarking: The Search for Industry Best Practices that Lead to Superior Performance. Part III: Why Benchmark?" *Quality Progress*, March 1989, pp. 76-82. (Reference #11846)

Camp, Robert C. "Benchmarking: The Search for Industry Best Practices that Lead to Superior Performance. Part IV: What to Benchmark." *Quality Progress*, April 1989, pp. 62-69. (Reference #10332)

Camp, Robert C. "Benchmarking: The Search for Industry Best Practices that Lead to Superior Performance. Part V: Beyond Benchmarking." *Quality Progress*, May 1989, pp. 66-68. (Reference #11848)

Camp, Robert C. "Competitive Benchmarking: Xerox's Powerful Quality Tool." From "Making Total Quality Happen," *The Conference Board Research Report #937*, 1990, pp. 35-42. (Reference #2697)

Carnevale, Ellen S. "On Target: From Expert to Expert Trainer." *Technical & Skills Training*, January 1992, pp. 30-33. (Reference #12191)

Case, John. "The Change Masters." *Inc.*, March 1992, pp. 58-70. (Reference #12143)

Cavinato, Joseph. "How to Benchmark Logistics Operations." *Distribution*, August 1988, pp. 93-96. (Reference #11778)

Cecil, Robert, and Ferraro, Richard. "IEs Fill Facilitator Role in Benchmarking Operations to Improve Performance." *Industrial Engineering*, Vol. 24, No. 4, April 1992, pp. 30-33. (Reference #12992)

"A CEO's Odyssey Toward World-Class Manufacturing." *Chief Executive*, September 1990, pp. 46-49. (Reference #11781)

Chase, Richard B., and Garvin, David A. "The Service Factory." *Harvard Business Review*, July-August 1989, pp. 61-69. (Reference #240)

Chitwood, Lera. "The People Chase." *Competitive Intelligence Review*, Winter 1992, pp. 25-27. (Reference #12782)

"Compensation & Expenses." *Sales & Marketing Management*, June 17, 1991, pp. 72-98. (Reference #11818)

"Competitive Benchmarking: A Practical Application." Xerox Corporation, 1990, 24 pages. (Reference #11794)

"Competitive Benchmarking: The Path to a Leadership Position." Xerox Corporation, 1988, 23 pages. (Reference #362)

"Competitive Benchmarking: What It Is and What It Can Do for You." Xerox Corporate Quality Office, May 1987, pp. 1-22. (Reference #1013)

Davis, Herbert W. "Physical Distribution Costs: Performance in Selected Industries, 1990." *Proceedings from the Council of Logistics Management Annual Conference*, October 7-10, 1990, pp. 65-72. (Reference #8992)

Delsanter, Judith M. "A Win-Win Situation." *The TQM Magazine*, Vol. 2, No. 3, July/August 1992, pp. 155-158. (Reference #12979)

DeToro, Irving J. "Strategic Planning for Quality at Xerox." *Quality Progress*, April 1987, pp. 16-20. (Reference #9116)

Dumaine, Brian. "Corporate Spies Snoop to Conquer." *Fortune*, November 1988, pp. 68-76. (Reference #10303)

Fahey, Paul P., and Ryan, Stephen. "Quality Begins and Ends with Data." *Quality Progress*, April 1992, pp. 75-79. (Reference #12625)

Fifer, Robert M. "Cost Benchmarking Functions in the Value Chain." *Planning Review*, May/June 1989, pp. 18-27. (Reference #2128)

Fleisher, Craig S., and Schoenfeld, Gerald A. "Functional-Level Competitive Intelligence: Human Resources Management." *Competitive Intelligence Review*, Winter 1992, pp. 2-7. (Reference #12553)

Foster, Thomas A. "Logistics Benchmarking: Searching for the Best." *Distribution*, Vol. 91, No. 3, March 1992, pp. 30-36. (Reference #12993)

Fuld, Leonard M. "Surveying Findings: Computer-Based Intelligence Systems Experience Growth and Problems." *Competitive Intelligence Review*, Winter 1992, pp. 31-33. (Reference #12781)

Fuld, Leonard M. "Taking the First Steps on the Path to Benchmarking." *Marketing News*, September 11, 1989, pp. 15, 20-21. (Reference #11849)

Furey, Timothy R. "Benchmarking: The Key to Developing Competitive Advantage in Mature Markets." *Planning Review*, September-October 1987, pp. 30-32. (Reference #11775)

Garvin, David A. "How the Baldrige Award Really Works." *Harvard Business Review*, November-December 1991, pp. 80-93. (Reference #11770)

Gass, Jerry. "Measure and Improve White-Collar Productivity." Measure & Improve White Collar Productivity Conference, New Orleans, December 14-15, 1989, 52 pages. (Reference #10728)

Geber, Beverly. "Benchmarking: Measuring Yourself Against the Best." *Training*, November 1990, pp. 36-44. (Reference #2416)

Ghoshal, Sumantra, and Westney, D. Eleanor. "Organizing Competitor Analysis Systems." *Strategic Management Journal*, Vol. 12, 1991, pp. 17-31. (Reference #11756)

Goff, Heidi R. "MasterCard Division Masters the Quality Possibilities." *National Productivity Review*, Winter 1991/1992, pp. 105-111. (Reference #12271)

Gold, Jacqueline S. "Return of the Native." *Financial World*, Vol. 161, No. 7, March 31, 1992, pp. 22-24. (Reference #12994)

Gordon, Jay. "Shippers Contain Transport Costs." *Distribution's Logistics Annual Report*, July 1990, pp. 26-29. (Reference #11346)

Graham, Scott. "Futurescape: Utilities Turn to Benchmarking." *Reddy News Sourcebook*, March 1991, pp. 18-22. (Reference #11779)

Grayson, C. Jackson. "Worldwide Competition." *The TQM Magazine*, Vol 2, No. 3, July/August 1992, pp. 134-138. (Reference #12974)

Guilmette, Harris, and Reinhart, Carlene. "Competitive Benchmarking: A New Concept for Training." *Training and Development Journal*, February 1984, pp. 70-71. (Reference #11850)

Harmon, Marion. "Benchmarking." *Quality Digest*, Vol. 12, No. 7, July 1992, pp. 20-31. (Reference #12980)

Hillmer, Steven C., and Trabelsi, Abdelwahed. "A Benchmarking Approach to Forecast Combination." *Journal of Business & Economic Statistics*, Vol. 7, No. 3, July 1989, pp. 353-362. (Reference #2139)

Hull, Darel R., and Tracy, Edward J. "AT&T Benchmarking: Fundamental Priority." *Proceedings from the Council of Logistics Management Annual Conference*, October 7-10, 1990, pp. 187-212. (Reference #8151)

"Improving Productivity Through Industry and Company Measurement." National Center for Productivity and Quality of Working Life, Series 2, October 1976, 77 pages. (Reference # 11254)

"In the Beginning There Was Competition." DuPont, 1990, 30 pages. (Reference #11508)

"Inter-Plant Comparisons: A Starting Point for Productivity Improvement." *APC Benchmarks*, May 1981, pp. 1-4. (Reference #2680)

Kahn, Zella L., and Packer, Michael B. "Total Factor Productivity for General Motors Corporation: 1975-1981." Technical Report, Productivity Research Program. Massachusetts Institute of Technology, 1982, 59 pages. (Reference #4008)

Kearns, David. "Xerox: Satisfying Customer Needs with a New Culture." *Management Review*, February 1989, pp. 61-63. (Reference #11851)

Kennedy, Carol. "Xerox Charts a New Strategic Direction." *Long Range Planning*, Vol. 22, No. 1, 1989, pp. 10-17. (Reference #2137)

Kokubo, Atsuro. "Japanese Competitive Intelligence for R&D." *Research/Technology Management*, Jan./Feb. 1992, pp. 33-34. (Reference #12879)

Kumar, Anil, and Sharman, Graham. "We Love Your Product, But Where Is It?" *Sloan Management Review*, Winter 1992, pp. 93-99. (Reference #11997)

Lee, Sang M.; Yoo, Sangjin; and Lee, Tosca M. "Korean Chaebols: Corporate Values and Strategies." *Organizational Dynamics*, Spring 1991, pp. 36-50. (Reference #11375)

A fascinating account of the development and operation of the major Korean enterprises. There are characteristics borrowed from both Japan and the United States, but Korean traditions and government procedures also play a vital role. These firms face a major test ahead with a recession in Korea, increased protectionism in some markets and increased domestic wage demands.

Lehman, William M. "A Strategic Alliance in Aerospace TQM Meets the Needs of the 1990s." *APICS*, May 1992, 2 pages. (Reference #12931)

Lewis, Jordan D. "Scanning for Opportunities." *Across the Board*, May 1990, pp. 53-57. (Reference #1666)

Lewontin, Sarah; Weiss, Fred; and Brandt, Robert. "IFMA Benchmarks Research." IFMA Conference 1990, October 28-31, 1990, pp. 149-172. (Reference #11493)

Lieberman, Marvin B., et al. "Firm-Level Productivity and Management Influence: A Comparison of U.S. and Japanese Automobile Producers." *Paper #1048*, Stanford University, Graduate School of Business, June 26, 1989, 34 pages. (Reference #10638)

Lorincz, Jim. "Purchasing Research: How Do You Measure Up?" *Purchasing World*, May 1990, pp. 30-33.

"Making Total Quality Happen." *Conference Board Research Report No. 937*, 1990, 90 pages. (Reference #3778)

Maturi, Richard J. "Benchmarking: The Search for Quality." *The Financial Manager*. March/April 1990, pp. 26-31. (Reference #2095)

McComas, Maggie; Knowlton, Christopher; and Langan, Patricia A. "Cutting Costs without Killing the Business." *Fortune*, October 13, 1986, pp. 70-78. (Reference #11780)

"Measuring R&D Effectiveness: A New Approach." *Manufacturing Competitiveness Frontiers*, January 1992, pp. 26-27. (Reference #12362)

Mitchell, Russell. "The Gap." *Business Week*, March 9, 1992, pp. 58-64. (Reference #12219)

Murdo, Pat. "Japan Keeps Thumb on Rising Health-Care Costs." *JEI Report*, No. 32B, August 17, 1990, pp. 4-8. (Reference #11311)

Nandi, S.N., et al. "Interfirm Comparison Revisited." *Productivity*, Vol. 32, No. 4, Jan./Mar. 1992, pp. 743-751. (Reference #12672)

"A National Benchmark Study on the Attitudes of the American Work Force." *Wyatt Work America*, 1989, 25 pages. (Reference #4688)

Nevens, T. Michael; Summe, Gregory L.; and Uttal, Bro. "Commercializing Technology: What the Best Companies Do." *Harvard Business Review*, May/June 1990, pp. 154-163. (Reference #11248)

Commercializing technology is portrayed as the key to success in the '90s, just as manufacturing excellence and total quality were the themes of the '80s. Commercialization involves system discipline more than inspiration; in fact, what these McKinsey Co. authors call commercialization covers most of the same components as standard total quality management applied to a high-tech organization that features cycle-time reduction and thorough market analysis. The authors emphasize benchmarking, cross-training, and "hands-on management."

Novich, Neil S. "Developing Superior Service as a Competitive Tool." Annual Conference Proceedings, Volume II, October 7-10, 1990, pp. 257-265. (Reference #7300)

Owen, Jean V. "Benchmarking World-Class Manufacturing." *Manufacturing Engineering*, March 1992, pp. 29-34. (Reference #12407)

Owen, Jean V. "Getting into the Benchmarking Game." *Manufacturing Engineering*, March 1992, p. 184. (Reference #12924)

Paich, Milo R. "Making Service Quality Look Easy." *Training*, February 1992, pp. 32-35. (Reference #12287)

Pipp, Frank J. "Management Commitment to Quality: Xerox Corporation." *Quality Progress*, August 1983, pp. 12-17. (Reference #11776)

Pontillo, Salvatore M. "Banking on Quality Improvement." *Quality Update*, Jan./ Feb. 1992, pp. 26-28. (Reference #12569)

"Productivity in Baking: Report I." Compiled by American Productivity Center. *Milling & Baking News*, May 31, 1983, pp. 34-48. (Reference #3159)

Pryor, Lawrence S. "Benchmarking: A Self-Improvement Strategy." *Journal of Business Strategy*, November-December 1989, pp. 28-32. (Reference #1673)

"Quality: Executive Priority or Afterthought?" *ASQC/Gallup Survey*, 1989, 80 pages. (Reference #2077)

"Recovering the Future at Xerox." *The Quality Executive*, July 1990, pp. 4-7. (Reference #2665)

"Report on Selected Financial Operating Ratios of Public Power Systems, 1986." American Public Power Association, June 1988, pp. 1-42. (Reference #109)

Rivest, Gerald. "Make Your Business More Competitive." *CMA Magazine*, May 1991, pp. 16-19. (Reference #9224)

This describes the value and operation of the Canadian government's Interfirm Comparison benchmarking program. Both financial and physical data are collected within each participating industry and measures of productivity and costs are created. The government works closely with each industry to interpret the data and stimulate corrective action.

"The Role of Competitive Intelligence for U.S. Competitiveness." *Competitive Intelligence Review*, Winter 1992, pp. 8-10. (Reference #12550)

Ruch, Daniel, and Roper, Janice John. "The Greening of Corporate Canada." *CMA Magazine*, Dec./Jan. 1992, pp. 15-18. (Reference #12837)

Ruggles, Richard, and Ruggles, Nancy D. "The Analysis of Longitudinal Establishment Data." Yale University, October 15, 1984, 86 pages. (Reference #8516)

"Sara Lee Direct: Not Held Hostage to 'Not Invented Here.'" *On Achieving Excellence*, June 1991, pp. 2-7. (Reference #11760)

Schmid, Robert E. "Reverse Engineering: A Service Product." *Planning Review*, September-October 1987, pp. 33-35. (Reference #11782)

Schreiber, Rita R. "The CIM Caper." *Manufacturing Engineering*, April 1989, pp. 85-89. (Reference #2125)

Scovel, Kathryn. "Learning from the Masters." *Human Resource Executive*, May 1991, pp. 28-29. (Reference #11852)

Shimoyamada, Kaoru. "The President's Audit: QC Audits at Komatsu." *Quality Progress*, January 1987, pp. 44-49. (Reference #9909)

Simon, Hermann. "Lessons from Germany's Midsize Giants." *Harvard Business Review*, March/April 1992, pp. 115-123. (Reference #12154)

Stalk, George; Evans, Philip; and Shulman, Lawrence E. "Competing on Capabilities: The New Rules of Corporate Strategy." *Harvard Business Review*, March/April 1992, pp. 57-69. (Reference #12159)

Tonkin, Lea. "Benchmarking Bound? Don't 'Just Do It.'" *Target*, Winter 1991, pp. 13-16. (Reference #11872)

Tonkin, Lea. "Unadorned Excellence: Stone Container Corporation, Corrugated Container Division, North Chicago, IL." *Target*, Summer 1991, pp. 32-40. (Reference #11768)

Tucker, Frances Gaither; Zivan, Seymour M.; and Camp, Robert C. "How to Measure Yourself Against the Best." *Harvard Business Review*, January-February, 1987, pp. 8-10. (Reference #11853)

Tyndall, Gene R. "How You Apply Benchmarking Makes All the Difference." *Marketing News*, November 12, 1990, pp. 18-19. (Reference #11725)

Vedder, James N. "How Much Can We Learn from Success?" *Journal of the Academy of Management Executives*, Vol. 6, No. 1, 1992, pp. 56-66. (Reference #12319)

Watson, Greg. "A Process for Competitive Edge." *TQM Magazine*, Vol 2, No. 3, July/August 1992, pp. 139-141. (Reference #12975)

Watson, Greg. "Competitive Analysis: Coordinate Competitive Analysis Tools to Get the Total Picture." *Productivity*, October 1991, pp. 8-9. (Reference #11880)

Weber, David O. "With a Reputation as One of the Nation's Most Productive Institutions, Forsyth Memorial Stresses Information, Participation, Trust, and Generous Rewards." *Healthcare Productivity Report*, March 1991, pp. 1-7. (Reference #10048)

Whately, Mark, and Aaron, Howard B. "Companies that Target World Class Are Destined to be Second Rate." *Quality Engineering*, Vol. 3, No. 2, 1990-1991, pp. 207-213. (Reference #11515)

Whiting, Rick. "Benchmarking: Lessons from the Best-in-Class." *Electronic Business*, October 7, 1991, pp. 128, 130, 132, 134. (Reference #11855)

Wilkerson, David; Kuh, Anne; and Wilkerson, Tracy. "A Tale of Change." *TQM Magazine*, Vol. 2, No. 3, July/August 1992, pp. 146-151. (Reference #12977)

Willding, Liz. "Use Benchmarking Methods to Become 'the Best of the Best.'" *TQC World*, Newsletter of Texas Instruments, September 1989, pp. 10-11. (Reference #11854)

Wood, Craig H.; Ritzman, Larry P.; and Sharma, Deven. "Strategic Information Management: Competitive Priorities and Manufacturing Performance Measures." *Proceedings from the Operations Management Association Conference*, 8th Annual, April 20-21, 1989, pp. 271-281. (Reference #11585)

Young, Steve, and Greenway, Brent. "Britain's Best Factories." *Management Today*, November 1990, pp. 76-89. (Reference #11791)

Appendixes

- A: The Benchmarking Code of Conduct
- B: Summary of the Deming Prize Application Checklist
- C: Summary of the 1991 Malcolm Baldrige National Quality Award Criteria
- D: Summary of the 1991 President's Award for Quality and Productivity
- E: Summary of the 1991 George M. Low Trophy Criteria (NASA's Productivity and Excellence Award)
- F: Summary of the 1991 Shingo Prize for Excellence in American Manufacturing Criteria
- G: Summary of the 1992 Malcolm Baldrige National Quality Award Criteria
- H: Baldrige Criteria Compared with ISO 9000

APPENDIX A
THE BENCHMARKING CODE OF CONDUCT

Preamble

Benchmarking — the process of identifying and learning from best practices anywhere in the world — is a powerful tool in the quest for continuous improvement.

To guide benchmarking encounters and to advance the professionalism and effectiveness of benchmarking, the International Benchmarking Clearinghouse, a service of the American Productivity & Quality Center, and the Strategic Planning Institute Council on Benchmarking have adopted this common Code of Conduct. We encourage all organizations to abide by this Code of Conduct. Adherence to these principles will contribute to efficient, effective, and ethical benchmarking. This edition of the Code of Conduct has been expanded to provide greater guidance on the protocol of benchmarking for beginners.

The Benchmarking Code of Conduct

Individuals agree for themselves and their company to abide by the following principles for benchmarking with other organizations.

1. Principle of Legality

- If there is any potential question on the legality of an activity, don't do it.
- Avoid discussions or actions that could lead to or imply an interest in restraint of trade, market, and/or customer allocation schemes, price fixing, dealing arrangements, bid rigging, or bribery. Don't discuss costs with competitors if costs are an element of pricing
- Refrain from the acquisition of trade secrets from any means that could be interpreted as improper, including the breach or inducement of a breach of any duty to maintain secrecy. Do not disclose or use any trade secret that may have been obtained through improper means or that was disclosed by another in violation of a duty to maintain its secrecy or limit its use.
- Do not, as a consultant or a client, extend one benchmarking study's findings to another company without first obtaining permission from the parties of the first study.

2. Principle of Exchange

- Be willing to provide the same type and level of information that you request from your benchmarking partner to your benchmarking partner.
- Communicate fully and early in the relationship to clarify expectations, avoid misunderstandings, and establish mutual interest in the benchmarking exchange.
- Be honest and complete.

3. Principle of Confidentiality

- Treat benchmarking interchange as confidential to the individuals and companies involved. Information must not be communicated outside the partnering organizations without the prior consent of the benchmarking partner who shared the information.
- A company's participation in a study is confidential and should not be communicated externally without its prior permission.

4. Principle of Use

- Use information obtained through benchmarking only for purposes of formulating improvement of operations or processes within the companies participating in the benchmarking study.
- The use or communication of a benchmarking partner's name with the data obtained or practices observed requires the prior permission of that partner.
- Do not use benchmarking as a means to market or sell.

5. Principle of First-Party Contact

- Initiate benchmarking contacts, whenever possible, through a benchmarking contact designated by the partner company.
- Respect the corporate culture of partner companies and work within mutually agreed upon procedures.
- Obtain mutual agreement with the designated benchmarking contact on any hand-off of communication or responsibility to other parties.

6. Principle of Third-Party Contact

- Obtain an individual's permission before providing his or her name in response to a contact request.
- Avoid communicating a contact's name in an open forum without the contact's permission.

7. Principle of Preparation

- Demonstrate commitment to the efficiency and effectiveness of benchmarking by completing preparatory work prior to making an initial benchmarking contact and following a benchmarking process.
- Make the most of your benchmarking partners' time by being fully prepared for each exchange.
- Help your benchmarking partners prepare by providing them with an interview guide or questionnaire and agenda prior to benchmarking visits.

8. Principle of Completion

- Follow through with each commitment made to your benchmarking partners in a timely manner.
- Complete each benchmarking study to the satisfaction of all benchmarking partners as mutually agreed.

9. Principle of Understanding and Action

- Understand how your benchmarking partners would like to be treated.
- Treat your benchmarking partners in the way that each benchmarking partner would like to be treated.
- Understand how each benchmarking partner would like to have the information he or she provides handled and used, and handle and use it in that manner.

APPENDIX B
SUMMARY OF THE DEMING PRIZE APPLICATION CHECKLIST

Item	Particulars
1. Policy	(1) Policies pursued for management, quality, and quality control (2) Method of establishing policies (3) Justifiability and consistency of policies (4) Utilization of statistical methods (5) Transmission and diffusion of policies (6) Review of policies and the results achieved (7) Relationship between policies and long- and short-term planning
2. Organization and Its Management	(1) Explicitness of the scopes of authority and responsibility (2) Appropriateness of delegations of authority (3) Interdivisional cooperation (4) Committees and their activities (5) Utilization of staff (6) Utilization of QC circle activities (7) Quality control diagnosis
3. Education and Dissemination	(1) Education programs and results (2) Quality- and control-consciousness, degrees of understanding of quality control (3) Teaching of statistical concepts and methods, and the extent of their dissemination (4) Grasp of the effectiveness of quality control

Item	Particulars
3. Education and Dissemination (cont.)	(5) Education of related company (particularly those in the same group, subcontractors, consignees, and distributors) (6) QC circle activities (7) System of suggesting ways of improvements and its actual conditions
4. Collection, Dissemination, and Use of Information on Quality	(1) Collection of external information (2) Transmission of information between divisions (3) Speed of information transmission (use of computers) (4) Data processing, statistical analysis of information, and utilization of the results
5. Analysis	(1) Selection of key problems and themes (2) Propriety of the analytical approach (3) Utilization of statistical methods (4) Linkage with proper technology (5) Quality analysis, process analysis (6) Utilization of analytical results (7) Assertiveness of improvement suggestions
6. Standardization	(1) Systematization of standards (2) Method of establishing, revising, and abolishing standards (3) Outcome of the establishment, revision, or abolition of standards (4) Contents of standards (5) Utilization of statistical methods (6) Accumulation of technology (7) Utilization of standards

Item	**Particulars**
7. Control	(1) Systems for control of quality and such related matters as cost and quantity
	(2) Control items and control points
	(3) Utilization of such statistical control methods as control charts and other statistical concepts
	(4) Contribution to performance of QC circle activities
	(5) Actual conditions of control activi-
8. Quality Assurance	(1) Procedure for the development of new products and services (analysis and upgrading of quality, checking of design, reliability, and other properties)
	(2) Safety and immunity from product liability
	(3) Process design, process analysis, and process control and improvement
	(4) Process capability
	(5) Instrumentation, gauging, testing, and inspecting
	(6) Equipment maintenance, and control of subcontracting, purchasing, and services
	(7) Quality assurance system and its audit
	(8) Utilization of statistical methods
	(9) Evaluation and audit of quality
	(10) Actual state of quality assurance
9. Results	(1) Measurement of results
	(2) Substantive results in quality, services, delivery, time, cost, profits, safety, environment, etc.

Item	**Particulars**
10. Planning for the Future	(1) Grasp of the present state of affairs and the concreteness of the plan
	(2) Measures for overcoming defects
	(3) Plans for further advances
	(4) Linkage with the long-term plans

For the entire set of Evaluation Criteria, please contact:

Deming Prize Committee
Union of Japanese Scientists and Engineers (JUSE)
5-10-11 Sendagaya, Shibuya-ku
Tokyo 151 JAPAN
Phone: (011)(81)(03) 5379-1227

APPENDIX C
SUMMARY OF THE 1991 MALCOLM BALDRIGE NATIONAL QUALITY AWARD CRITERIA

1991 Examination Categories/Items	Points
1.0 Leadership	
1.1 Senior Executive Leadership	40
1.2 Quality Values	15
1.3 Management for Quality	25
1.4 Public Responsibility	20
2.0 Information and Analysis	
2.1 Scope and Management of Quality Data and Information	20
2.2 Competitive Comparisons and Benchmarks	30
2.3 Analysis of Quality Data and Information	20
3.0 Strategic Quality Planning	
3.1 Strategic Quality Planning Process	35
3.2 Quality Goals and Plans	25
4.0 Human Resource Utilization	
4.1 Human Resource Management	20
4.2 Employee Involvement	40
4.3 Quality Education and Training	40
4.4 Employee Recognition and Performance Measurement	25
4.5 Employee Well-Being and Morale	25
5.0 Quality Assurance of Products and Services	
5.1 Design and Introduction of Quality Products and Services	35
5.2 Process Quality Control	20
5.3 Continuous Improvement of Processes	20
5.4 Quality Assessment	15
5.5 Documentation	10
5.6 Business Process and Support Service Quality	20
5.7 Supplier Quality	20
6.0 Quality Results	
6.1 Product and Service Quality Results	90
6.2 Business Process, Operational, and Support Service Quality Results	50
6.3 Supplier Quality Results	40

1991 Examination Categories/Items   **Points**

7.0   Customer Satisfaction

7.1   Determining Customer Requirements and Expectations   30
7.2   Customer Relationship Management   50
7.3   Customer Service Standards   20
7.4   Commitment to Customers   15
7.5   Complaint Resolution for Quality Improvement   25
7.6   Determining Customer Satisfaction   20
7.7   Customer Satisfaction Results   70
7.8   Customer Satisfaction Comparison   70

Total Points   **1000**

For the entire set of Evaluation Criteria, please contact:

Malcolm Baldrige National Quality Award
National Institute of Standards and Technology
Route 270 and Quince Orchard Road
Administration Building, Room A537
Gaithersburg, MD 20899
Phone: (301) 975-2036

APPENDIX D
SUMMARY OF THE 1991 PRESIDENT'S AWARD FOR
QUALITY AND PRODUCTIVITY CRITERIA

Evaluation Criteria Elements (Improvement Criteria)

1.	Top-Management Leadership and Support	20
2.	Strategic Planning	15
3.	Focus on the Customer	40
4.	Employee Training and Recognition	15
5.	Employee Empowerment and Teamwork	15
6.	Measurement and Analysis	15
7.	Quality Assurance	30
8.	Quality and Productivity Improvement Results	50
Total Points		**200**

For the entire set of Evaluation Criteria, please contact:

The Federal Quality Institute
United States Office of Personnel Management
Washington, DC 20044-0099
Phone: (202) 376-3747

APPENDIX E
SUMMARY OF THE 1991 GEORGE M. LOW TROPHY CRITERIA
(NASA'S PRODUCTIVITY AND EXCELLENCE AWARD)

Evaluation Criteria Elements	Points
1.0 Performance Achievements and Improvements	
1.1 Customer Satisfaction	
1.1.1 Contact Performance	130
1.1.2 Schedule	50
1.1.3 Cost	50
1.2 Quality	
1.2.1 Quality Assurance (hardware/software/service)	120
1.2.2 Vendor quality assurance and improvement	50
1.2.3 Reporting and communication	40
1.2.4 Problem prevention and resolution	40
1.3 Productivity	
1.3.1 Software utilization	40
1.3.2 Process improvement and equipment modernization	30
1.3.3 Resources conservation	20
1.3.4 Efficient use of manpower	30
2.0 Process Achievements and Improvements	
2.1 Commitment and Communication	
2.1.1 Top-management commitment/involvement	100
2.1.2 Goals, planning, implementation, and measurement	80
2.1.3 Communication	40
2.2 Human Resource Activities	
2.2.1 Training	50
2.2.2 Work force involvement	50
2.2.3 Awards and recognition	40
2.2.4 Health and safety	40
Total Points	**1000**

For the entire set of Evaluation Criteria, please contact:

NASA Quality and Productivity Improvements Program Office
NASA Headquarters — Code QB
Washington, DC 20546
Phone: (202) 453-8415

APPENDIX F
SUMMARY OF THE 1991 SHINGO PRIZE FOR EXCELLENCE IN AMERICAN MANUFACTURING CRITERIA

Evaluation Criteria Elements (Evaluation Criteria)	Percent
I. Strategic Leadership, Involvement and Support	
A. Management Leadership	10%
B. Employee Involvement	10%
C. Business Process, Operations, and Support Service Improvement	10%
II. Manufacturing Methods, Systems, and Processes	40%
III. Measured Improvements in Productivity, Quality, and Customer Satisfaction	
A. Productivity	10%
B. Quality	10%
C. Customer Satisfaction	10%
IV. Summary of Achievements	
V. Future Vision/Direction	
Total Percentage	**100%**

For the entire set of Evaluation Criteria, please contact:

The Shingo Prize
College of Business
Utah State University
Logan, UT 84322-3521
Phone: (801) 750-2281

APPENDIX G:
SUMMARY OF THE 1992 MALCOLM BALDRIGE
NATIONAL QUALITY AWARD CRITERIA

1992 Examination Categories/Items	Points
1.0 Leadership	
1.1 Senior Executive Leadership	45
1.2 Management for Quality	25
1.3 Public Responsibility	20
2.0 Information and Analysis	
2.1 Scope and Management of Quality and Performance Data and Information	15
2.2 Competitive Comparisons and Benchmarks	25
2.3 Analysis and Uses of Company-Level Data	40
3.0 Strategic Quality Planning	
3.1 Strategic Quality and Company Performance Planning Process	35
3.2 Quality and Performance Plans	25
4.0 Human Resource Development and Management	
4.1 Human Resource Management	20
4.2 Employee Involvement	40
4.3 Employee Education and Training	40
4.4 Employee Performance and Recognition	25
4.5 Employee Well-Being and Morale	25

1992 Examination Categories/Items		Points
5.0	**Management of Process Quality**	
5.1	Design and Introduction of Quality Products and Services	40
5.2	Process Management — Product and Service Production and Delivery Processes	35
5.3	Process Management — Business Processes and Support Services	30
5.4	Supplier Quality	20
5.5	Quality Assessment	15
6.0	**Quality and Operational Results**	
6.1	Product and Service Quality Results	75
6.2	Company Operational Results	45
6.3	Business Process and Support Service Results	25
6.4	Supplier Quality Results	35
7.0	**Customer Focus and Satisfaction**	
7.1	Customer Relationship Management	65
7.2	Commitment to Customers	15
7.3	Customer Satisfaction Determination	35
7.4	Customer Satisfaction Results	75
7.5	Customer Satisfaction Comparison	75
7.6	Future Requirements and Expectations of Customers	35
Total Points		**1000**

For the entire set of Evaluation Criteria, please contact:

Malcolm Baldrige National Quality Award
National Institute of Standards and Technology
Route 270 and Quince Orchard Road
Administration Building, Room A537
Gaithersburg, MD 20899
Phone: (301) 975-2036

APPENDIX H
BALDRIGE CRITERIA COMPARED WITH ISO 9000

A first step toward understanding how to integrate ISO 9000 with a TQM program is to compare the ISO 9004 Quality System Guidelines with the 1991 assessment criteria of the Baldrige Award. By comparing these systems, we can better appreciate the type of quality system that is needed to integrate conformance quality and perceived quality into an overall quality approach.

1991 Baldrige	ISO 9004	Examination Item
1.1		Senior Executive Leadership
	4.1	Management Responsibility – General
	18.1.2	Executive and Management Training
	5.5	Review and Evaluation of Quality System
1.2		Quality Values
	4.2	Quality Policy
	4.4	Quality System
1.3		Management for Quality
	4.3	Quality Objectives
	4.4	Quality System
	5.1	Quality System Principles – Quality Loop
	5.2	Structure of the Quality System
	6.0	Economics — Quality-Related Costs
	6.4	Management Visibility
1.4	NA	Public Responsibility
2.1		Scope and Management of Quality Data and Information
	5.3.4	Quality Records
	9.8	Receiving Quality Records
	17.3	Quality Records
	18.3.4	Measuring Quality

1991 Baldrige	ISO 9004	Examination Item
2.2	NA	Competitive Comparisons and Benchmarks
2.3		Analysis of Quality Data and Information
	20.0	Use of Statistical Methods
3.1	NA	Strategic Quality Planning Process
3.2		Quality Goals and Plans
	4.3	Quality Objectives
4.1	NA	Human Resource Management
4.2	18.3	Motivation
4.3		Quality Education and Training
	18.2	Qualification
	18.1	Personnel Training
4.4	NA	Employee Recognition and Performance Measurement
4.5	NA	Employee Well-Being and Morale
5.1		Design and Introduction of Quality Products and Services
	8.0	Quality in Specification and Design

1991 Baldrige	ISO 9004	Examination Item
5.2		Process Quality Control
	9.0	Quality in Procurement
	10.0	Quality in Production
	11.0	Control of Production
	12.0	Product Verification
	13.0	Control of Measuring and Test Equipment
	14.0	Nonconformity
	15.0	Corrective Action
5.3	NA	Continuous Improvement Process
5.4		Quality Assessment
	5.4	Auditing the Quality System
	5.5	Review and Evaluation of the Quality Documentation and Records
5.5		Documentation
	5.3	Documentation of the Quality System
	17.0	Quality Documentation and Records
5.6		Business Process and Support Service Quality
	16.0	Handling and Post-Production Functions
5.7		Supplier Quality
	9.0	Quality in Procurement
6.1	NA	Product and Service Quality Results
6.2	NA	Business Process, Operational, and Support Service Quality Results
6.3	NA	Supplier Quality Results

1991 Baldrige	ISO 9004	Examination Item
7.1		Determining Customer Requirements and Expectations
	7.0	Quality in Marketing
7.2		Customer Relationship Management
	16.3	Marketing Reporting and Product Supervision
7.3		Customer Service Standards
	16.2	After-Sales Servicing
7.4		Commitment to Customers
	19.0	Product Safety and Liability
7.5		Complaint Resolution for Quality Improvement
	16.3	Marketing Reporting and Product Supervision
7.6	NA	Determining Customer Satisfaction
7.7	NA	Customer Satisfaction Results
7.8	NA	Customer Satisfaction Comparison

For copies of the ASQC/ANSI Q-90 Series (ISO Documents in the American version), please contact:

The American Society for Quality Control
611 East Wisconsin Avenue
P.O. Box 3005
Milwaukee, WI 53201-3005
Phone: (414) 272-8375

About the Author

The American Productivity & Quality Center, founded in 1977, is a nonprofit organization that works with business, labor, government, and academia to improve productivity, quality, and quality of work life. With support from over 400 founders, sponsors, and members, the Center provides a broad range of advisory, research, and information services. The Center is based in Houston.

The Center's International Benchmarking Clearinghouse was established in 1992 to help organizations improve quality and productivity through learning from best practices worldwide. Its mission is to provide benchmarking information and services as well as to continuously improve the benchmarking process.

OTHER BOOKS FROM PRODUCTIVITY PRESS

Productivity Press publishes and distributes materials on continuous improvement in productivity, quality, and the creative involvement of all employees. Many of our products are direct source materials from Japan that have been translated into English for the first time and are available exclusively from Productivity. Supplemental products and services include membership groups, conferences, seminars, in-house training and consulting, audio-visual training programs, and industrial study missions. Call toll-free 1-800-394-6868 for our free catalog.

Hoshin Kanri
Policy Deployment for Successful TQM

Yoji Akao (ed.)

Hoshin kanri, the Japanese term for policy deployment, is an approach to strategic planning and quality improvement that has become a pillar of Total Quality Management (TQM) for a growing
number of U.S. firms. This book is a compilation of examples of policy deployment that demonstrates how company vision is converted into individual responsibility. It includes practical
guidelines, 150 charts and diagrams, and five case studies that illustrate the procedures of hoshin kanri. The six steps to advanced process planning are reviewed and include a five-year vision, one-year plan, deployment to departments, execution, monthly audit, and annual audit.
ISBN 0-915299-57-7 / 256 pages / $65.00 / Order HOSHIN-B134

Quality Function Deployment
Integrating Customer Requirements into Product Design

Yoji Akao (ed.)

Written by the creator of QFD, this book provides direct source material on one of the essential tools for world class manufacturing. More and more companies are using QFD to identify customer requirements, translate them into quantified quality characteristics, and then build them into their products and services. This casebook introduces the concept of quality deployment as it has been applied in a variety of industries in Japan.
ISBN 0-915299-41-0 / 387 pages / $85.00 / Order QFD-B134

Handbook for Productivity Measurement and Improvement

William F. Christopher and Carl G. Thor, eds.

An unparalleled resource! In over 100 chapters, nearly 80 front-runners in the quality movement reveal the evolving theory and specific practices of world-class organizations. Spanning a wide variety of industries and business sectors, they discuss quality and productivity in manufacturing, service industries, profit centers, administration, nonprofit and government institutions, health care and education. Contributors include Robert C. Camp, Peter F. Drucker, Jay W. Forrester, Joseph M. Juran, Robert S. Kaplan, John W. Kendrick, Yasuhiro Monden, and Lester C. Thurow. Comprehensive in scope and organized for easy reference, this compendium belongs in every company and academic institution concerned with business and industrial viability.
ISBN 1-56327-007-2 / 1344 pages / $90.00 / Order HPM-B134

Productivity Press, Inc., Dept. BK, P.O. Box 13390, Portland, OR 97213 Telephone: 1-800-394-6868   Fax: 1-800-394-6286

The Teamwork Advantage
An Inside Look at Japanese Product and Technology Development
Jeffrey L. Funk

How are so many Japanese manufacturing firms shortening product time-to-market, reducing costs, and improving quality? The answer is teamwork. Dr. Funk spent 18 months as a visiting
engineer at Mitsubishi and Yokogawa Hokushin Electric and knows firsthand how Japanese corporate culture promotes effective teamwork in production, design, and technology development.
Here's a penetrating case study and analysis that presents a truly viable model for the West.
ISBN 0-915299-69-0 / 508 pages / $49.95 / Order TEAMAD-B134

The Visual Factory
Building Participation Through Shared Information
Michel Greif

If you're aware of the tremendous improvements achieved in productivity and quality as a result of employee involvement, then you'll appreciate the great value of creating a visual factory. This book shows how visual management can make the factory a place where workers and supervisors freely communicate and take improvement action. It details how to develop meeting and communication areas, communicate work standards and instructions, use visual production controls such as kanban, and make goals and progress visible. Includes more than 200 diagrams
and photos.
ISBN 0-915299-67-4 / 305 pages / $55.00 / Order VFAC-B134

Concurrent Engineering
Shortening Lead Times, Raising Quality, and Lowering Costs
John R. Hartley

By simultaneously taking into account the concerns of design, production, purchasing, finance, and marketing from the very first stages of product planning, concurrent engineering makes doing it right the first time the rule instead of the exception. An introductory handbook, this text gives managers 16 clear guidelines for achieving concurrent engineering and provides abundant case studies of Japanese, U.S., and European successes.
ISBN 1-56327-006-4 / 330 pages / $60.00 / Order CONC-B134

Canon Production System
Creative Involvement of the Total Workforce
compiled by the Japan Management Association

A fantastic success story! Canon set a goal to increase productivity by three percent per month and achieved it! The first book-length case study to show how to combine the most effective Japanese management principles and quality improvement techniques into one overall strategy that improves every area of the company on a continual basis.
ISBN 0-915299-06-2 / 256 pages / $39.95 / Order CANON-B134

Kanban and Just-In-Time at Toyota
Management Begins at the Workplace

Japan Management Association
Translated by David J. Lu

Toyota's world-renowned success proves that with kanban, the Just-In-Time production system (JIT) makes most other manufacturing practices obsolete. This simple but powerful classic is based on seminars given by JIT creator Taiichi Ohno to introduce Toyota's own supplier companies to JIT. It shows how to implement the world's most efficient production system. A clear and complete introduction.
ISBN 0-915299-48-8 / 211 pages / $39.95 / Order KAN-B134

Measuring, Managing, and Maximizing Performance

Will Kaydos

You do not need to be an exceptionally skilled technician or inspirational leader to improve your company's quality and productivity. In non-technical, jargon-free, practical terms this book details the entire process of improving performance, from why and how the improvement process work to what must be done to begin and to sustain continuous improvement of performance. Special emphasis is given to the role that performance measurement plays in identifying problems and opportunities.
ISBN 0-915299-98-4 / 304 pages / $39.95 / Order MMMP-B134

20 Keys to Workplace Improvement

Iwao Kobayashi

This easy-to-read introduction to the "20 keys" system presents an integrated approach to assessing and improving your company's competitive level. The book focuses on systematic improvement through five levels of achievement in such primary areas as industrial housekeeping, small group activities, quick changeover techniques, equipment maintenance, and computerization. A scoring guide is included, along with information to help plan a strategy for your company's world class improvement effort.
ISBN 0-915299-61-5 / 264 pages / $39.95 / Order 20KEYS-B134

Corporate Planning and Policy Design
A System Dynamics Approach (3rd ed.)

James M. Lyneis

System dynamics is a tool for planning and policy design that provides insight into the many critical problem areas in growing companies, including underperformance, production and inventory instability, improving response to growth, product shortages, labor instability, lost market share, adverse consequences of financial control of inventory, and excess capacity. See how this remarkable tool for corporate planning can work for your organization.
ISBN 0-262-12083-6 / 520 pages / $44.95 / Order XCPPD-B134

Performance Measurement for World Class Manufacturing
A Model for American Companies
Brian H. Maskell

If your company is adopting world class manufacturing techniques, you'll need new methods of performance measurement to control production variables. In practical terms, this book describes the new methods of performance measurement and how they are used in a changing environment. For manufacturing managers as well as cost accountants, it provides a theoretical foundation of these innovative methods supported by extensive practical examples. The book specifically addresses performance measures for delivery, process time, production flexibility, quality, and finance.
ISBN 0-915299-99-2 / 448 pages / $55.00 / Order PERFM-B134

A New American TQM
Four Practical Revolutions in Management
Shoji Shiba, Alan Graham, and David Walden

For TQM to succeed in America, you need to create an American-style "learning organization" with the full commitment and understanding of senior managers and executives. Written expressly for this audience, A New American TQM offers a comprehensive and detailed explanation of TQM and how to implement it, based on courses taught at MIT's Sloan School of Management and the Center for Quality Management, a consortium of American hi-tech companies. Full of case studies and amply illustrated, the book examines major quality tools and how they are being used by the most progressive American companies today.
ISBN 1-56327-032-3 / 500 pages / $49.95 / Order NATQM-xxx

Vision Management
Translating Strategy into Action
SANNO Management Development Research Center (ed.)

For over ten years, managers of Japan's top companies have gathered at SANNO University to brainstorm about innovative corporate management methods. This book is based on the proven methodology that evolved from their ideas. It describes how the intangible aspects of vision-based strategy can be integrated into a concrete implementation model and clarifies the relationship among vision, strategy, objectives, goals, and day-to-day activities.
ISBN 0-915299-80-1 / 272 pages / $29.95 / Order VISM-B134

The Benchmarking Workbook
Adapting Best Practices for Performance Improvement
Gregory H. Watson

Managers today need benchmarking to anticipate trends and maintain competitive advantage. This practical workbook shows you how to do your own benchmarking study. Watson's discussion includes a case study that takes you through each step of the benchmarking process, raises thought-provoking questions, and provides examples of how to use forms for a benchmarking study.
ISBN 1-56327-033-1 / 169 pages / $29.95 / Order BENCHW-B134

Productivity Press, Inc., Dept. BK, P.O. Box 13390, Portland, OR 97213 Telephone: 1-800-394-6868   Fax: 1-800-394-6286

Demass
Transforming the Dinosaur Corporation

M. M. Stuckey

This eye-opening new book shows how inside many of America's manufacturing giants, sheer size — massiveness — has become an obstacle to staying competitive. Demassification, or "demass," is the structural remedy to the inflexibility and relatively slow time-to-market of these giant corporations. This book provides a model for radical decentralization and improved speed-to-market with a thorough description of the demass process, what is needed for its implementation, and a study of successful demass at Eastman Kodak.

ISBN 1-56327-042-0 / 283 pages / $24.95 / Order DEMASS-B134

TO ORDER: Write, phone, or fax Productivity Press, Dept. BK, P.O. Box 13390, Portland, OR 97213, phone 1-800-394-6868, fax 1-800-394-6286. Send check or charge to your credit card (American Express, Visa, MasterCard accepted).

U.S. ORDERS: Add $5 shipping for first book, $2 each additional for UPS surface delivery. Add $5 for each AV program containing 1 or 2 tapes; add $12 for each AV program containing 3 or more tapes. We offer attractive quantity discounts for bulk purchases of individual titles; call for more information

INTERNATIONAL ORDERS: Write, phone, or fax for quote and indicate shipping method desired. Prepayment in U.S. dollars must accompany your order (checks must be drawn on U.S. banks). When quote is returned with payment, your order will be shipped promptly by the method requested.